All About
Darts

America's most complete and up-to-date book on the game of darts

I.L. Brackin and W. Fitzgerald

CB

CONTEMPORARY
BOOKS

CHICAGO

Published by Contemporary Books, Inc.
Two Prudential Plaza, Chicago, Illinois 60601-6790
Manufactured in the United States of America
Library of Congress Catalog Card Number: 76-29366
International Standard Book Number: 0-8092-4984-7

TABLE OF CONTENTS

———

Acknowledgements

It's difficult to write a book late at night in a crowded bar, especially when you are just a few feet away from the darts board. The perseverance required to write night after night was surpassed only by some of the darts records noted in this book. We therefore dedicate this book primarily to ourselves, without whose efforts this book would not be.

We must acknowledge, however, the special contributions of many others. Our special thanks to:

* Masayo Ito for her incredible perception of darts players' peculiarities and her patience in drawing the cartoons in this book.

* Sweetie Morioka for her hours and hours of labor on the typewriter and devotion to our cause.

* Maurice Anderson for his undying faith that the book would eventually be completed and for his many valuable suggestions.

* Merle Hinrichs for his we know not what.

* Peter Welch, our historian and statistician, who knew how many pig hairs it takes to make one dart board: 1,753,212 hairs from a white pig, 2,955,813 from a black pig, 517,327 from a bright red pig, and 485,603 from a green pig.

Special thanks also are due to *Darts World* magazine of England for allowing us to use material published in its pages. Guiness Superlatives Limited for giving us their kind permission to reproduce darts records from their *Guiness Book of Records*. The *News of the World* newspaper of Great Britain for information and records of their annual World Championships.

Any resemblance the cartoons may bear to actual people, living or just passing through, is probably coincidental.

Ivan Brackin
William Fitzgerald

Introduction

Darts is one of the most exciting indoor sports you can play with your clothes on. More important, it is one of the most interesting and intensely competive indoor sports of them all.

Even a veteran player would be hard put to find a straight answer to the question. "How do you play darts?" The scope of the sport for variety and skill would fill a whole book. This is it.

There is information in this book of value to both the expert and the beginner. It describes not only how to play darts and the many different games, but also how to play darts better.

We hope you enjoy reading it as much as we have enjoyed compiling it.

CHAPTER 1

How it all started

"Ang Ye Board on That Thar Rock, Father."

The English believe the game of darts arrived in America with the Pilgrims at Plymouth Rock. But as every American knows, the Indians had their own game of "arrows" centuries before the Pilgrims landed.

It is recorded that the Pilgrims did in fact bring their own "dartes" with them and since the game never really became popular until recently we can assume they were soundly beaten at it by the Indians during their first few games here, so abandoned it.

Meanwhile, in England and very much so in Ireland, the darts game grew slowly throughout the centuries and British perserverance gradually developed it into the present exciting sport played by millions of people around the world (an estimated 7 million regulars in Britain alone).

If the British had invented gunpowder . . .

History books tell us that darts originated from a warriors' pastime. In respites between battles the bored soldiers, far from their wives, girlfriends and wenches, occupied themselves with other manly pursuits, one of which was competing against each other by hurling short throwing spears into the upturned ends of wine barrels, empty ones presumably, or into quintains. If they had invented guns sooner the game may never have progressed.

As their pleasant pastime became a competitive sport, natural progression and a shortage of wine barrels called for a more critically marked target. The answer was

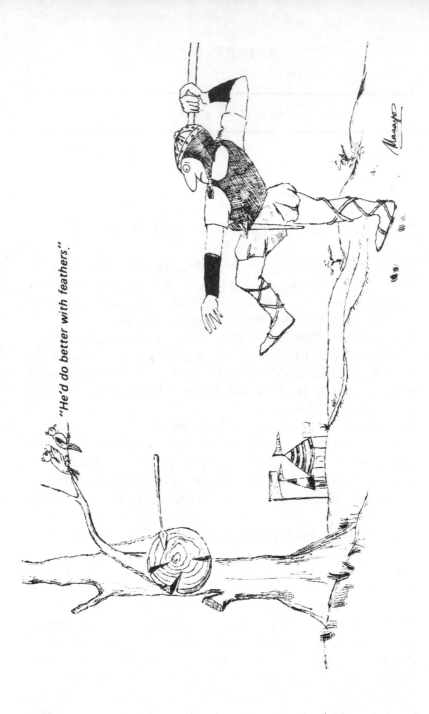

"He'd do better with feathers".

found by taking a round slice of a felled tree and hanging it up to provide a graded target. The natural concentric rings of the tree proved ideal for scoring purposes while the cracks which appeared as the wood dried out gave the radial lines for selection of score areas. Here we see the beginnings of our carefully spoked modern dartboard. During the long English winter nights the boards were moved indoors by the fire hearth. Restricted space indoors led to shorter darts being adopted and basic indoor games rules established. Perhaps some of these first games still exist as it is almost impossible to trace the origins of many of today's games and customs. In time, landlords became sponsors of the sport and cut their own log ends and by the late eighteenth century the first dartboard manufacturers had appeared, men who were probably on the business end of the wood cutting industry.

Luckily for the modern darts player the game was not one of the many sports banned during the suppressive reigns of the Middle Ages. Darts was considered a sport of military mien and useful for keeping soldiers' throwing arms in practice. The Dark Ages were therefore a fairly bright time for ye olde dartes.

As hurling darts became more widespread under official sanction it apparently graduated from the ranks. Regimental competition increased, officers, and later even nobility picked up the game, so very soon cries of "mugs away" could be heard echoing through the stone corridors of many a lord's castle. It is an historical fact that Ann Boleyn gave a set of darts to King Henry VIII though the story that she lost her head when she beat him has not been verified.

The game maintained its military affiliations through to the establishment of the British Empire when soldiers' drinking clubs with their built-in dartboards stretched all the way from Brighton to Burma. Locals in many countries adopted the sport but the British players remained dominant until very recently.

In the meantime, as most British soldiers and sailors were overseas conquering and maintaining new territory for the Crown the game was going through a slump back home,

"Mugs Away, M'Lord"

only being played in a few taverns. It wasn't until the beginning of the 20th century that the game of darts began its rapid climb towards the popularity it has today. The sport took to the air at one stage of the First World War when men sat in the cockpits of their flying machines armed with steel darts and hunted the skies of Europe for Zeppelins. They became very proficient marksmen and besides puncturing the gas bags of quite a few Zeppelins began hurling their projectiles with great accuracy into German trenches. It must have been terrifying to see a biplane screaming down with an airman sighting a vicious steel dart at your middle. At this time it was rumoured that every farmer along the Rhine kept his bull indoors.

There was a danger of darts as we know it today being replaced by some other similiar game as variations appeared around the country — even a blowpipe version using a miniature board was being played in the taverns of south England at the end of the last century. Some Scandinavians still play the game with foot long arrows from several yards distance.

Since the turn of the century the sport has twice defeated attempts by magistrates to have it banned. In 1908 a courtroom game convinced the magistrate that darts was indeed a game of skill and not of 'chance' in which case it could be played legally in taverns. The sport was actually banned for a short period in Scotland when local magistrates decided it had a corrupting influence. The resulting public outcry eventually reached the ears of the Home Secretary in London who stepped up to the line and told the· magistrates where they could throw their ban.

Standardization of equipment, in an age where everything was becoming standardized soon established the modern game as the pub game and brought about a greater aspect of skill to the contest.

Today, Britain is still the center of world darts with over seven million players and seven thousand registered clubs. The liberated women of Britain have formed more than four hundred clubs of their own and comprise a regular part of contests including participation in mixed doubles. America is fast catching up. Latest estimates count well over a million adherents in the U.S.A. plus many more occasional "chuckers". More than three hundred thousand dartboards are being sold annually and despite the fewer numbers, top players are often more than a match for their British counterparts. Competition purses now run into the tens of thousands of dollars, providing an irresistible incentive for new players.

> There are more pubs with dartboards in the center of New York than there are in the center of London.

There is talk, mostly among darts players, of including the sport in the Olympics. Why not? A headcount would probably show that there are a hundred times more men and women in the world throwing darts than shooting clay pigeons or splashing around in kayaks. Archery, a mechanically assisted method of projecting darts, has returned to the Olympics after an absence of over fifty years. Darts is a close cousin and requires no less, perhaps even more, individual skill. Inclusion in the Olympics would be a tremendous boost to the game and it would create a new international contest arena. In addition, it would help to standardize equipment and game rules, while at the same time win for the sport millions more participants around the world.

What has made this ancient sport from across the Atlantic suddenly so popular?

It is simple. Ask any newcomer to pick up three darts and throw them at the center of the board. Missed? Try again . . . and again . . . And so we have another darts player joining the swelling ranks of those folk who will always have the next three darts ahead of them.

A recent national darts competition in Britain attracted the participation of players from over 40,000 pubs. *That's a lot of pubs.*

You don't have to be a beer drinker to play darts, but it helps.

At Derby, in England, a darts team was suddenly expelled from their local pub and their darts league, in which they were champions. The reason: the team didn't drink enough beer. The landlord ordered them out of his pub for poor beer consumption and they were then banned from the darts league for conduct unbecoming the beery traditions of the game. This story is true, so let it stand as a warning. Not every darts player has to be a beer drinker, (the ladies may prefer mixed), but the idea is to point out the historical relationship the two have always enjoyed. Look at the Old Country's major tournaments and you find them studded with names like Bass-charington, Whitbread, Watney Mann, Double Diamond, and Tetleys, all major sponsors, all breweries.
Places like the Brown Bear, the White House, the Star & Garter, the Lincoln Arms, Cotton Tree Inn... all famous pubs, are renowned not particularly for their location or decor but for the very high standards of their resident darts teams.

Some of the world's best darts players *are* fitness freaks but even they agree that a few beers help relax the nerves and steady the hand. *A few more beers, however, and accuracy plummets.*

Open the door of any darts establishment and the first thing to hit you will be the strong smell of beer. Either that or dart.

7

A quarter-finalist in the 1973 international championships weighed a healthy two-hundred sixty-four pounds.

Why do darts and beer make such perfect partners? The bulk of today's players are men who have chosen their sport after very careful consideration of all the alternatives.

A beer belly for instance may have weighed heavily in their decision. To the darts player a beer belly is no hindrance, as it most certainly is in many other sports. All he has to do is lift his arm every so often, walk to the board, and retrieve his darts. On the contrary, a beer belly is undoubtedly a tremendous advantage, lowering the body's center of gravity, discouraging sway, and anchoring the legs and feet solidly to the mat while throwing.

Some of today's sports are simply too strenuous for the devoted beer drinker. Joggling all that beer around in the belly while running stooped over with a heavy bowling ball makes little medical sense. Golf is no friend of the inveterate guzzler. The stretch of countryside to the 19th hole can be a vast Sahara when his six-pack ran out on the 12th.

No, darts is the answer, and you will never find a veteran darts player very far away from his glass. Elbow on the bar, foot on the rail, a fistful of darts, a beer within easy reach and you have a happy man awaiting his turn at the board, all set for an unstrenuous evening.

Some players even carry their glasses with them while throwing, often a sign that they don't trust their friends or an indication of basic psychological insecurity. This is not recommended. Spillage can create a hazard in the way of a slippery mat, often leading to a lawsuit. Chalk powder falling from the scoreboard into a beer glass may rouse all sorts of latent stomach ailments.

What other sport offers the chance to stand around drinking beer with your friends while engaging in skilful and often fierce competition?

No matter how the tension builds up it can always be washed away, or at least temporarily stayed, with a fresh round of beers. At darts you can lounge. Nobody is going to ask you to perform feats of physical courage, leap around a court or dash after a ball, in fact the more relaxed you are the better you are likely to throw. Some darts players get so relaxed they actually fall flat on their faces after rounding off a game by throwing a shattering score. There is a two-hundred-pound player from the East Coast who refuses to throw any darts until he's drained the contents of at least six bottles of beer. Even then he is still hopeless until he has seen the back of another six bottles. By this time he will have reached a peak of absolute brilliance before his final collapse. He can actually time himself to reach this peak when all the heavy gambling takes place, then pretends to go to sleep on the bar after cleaning everybody out. No cajoling can get him to play another game, even though strong men have tried to hold him up while he throws.

How to qualify as a darts player

A Mrs. Turner of England broke her ankle and dislocated her shoulder during a local match of darts. She gallantly finished the match while supported by two friends.
That's what friends are for.

A highly competitive, skillful, exciting, physical sport and you can play it **without** having to do any of the following:

getting bruised
dashing 100 yards in 10 seconds
staying sober
walking 4 miles with a heavy bag
getting wet
giving up smoking
taking a shower with the boys

Darts is a sport for everybody. To play it here's what you **don't** need:

a ball
long legs
short legs
webbed feet
muscles
big fists
a left lung
two eyes
fast reflexes
a bank account
2 days leave
a license
a woman
a high IQ

Onwards, to the more serious aspects of our sport.

CHAPTER II

Equipment

The dartboard

No game is complete without one.
In the beginning, there was the lump of wood, and from it, through the maelstrom of darts history was developed the modern dartboard, known as the 'Clock', and all its cousins. As you will learn later in this chapter, lumps of wood, cork, paper and even clay are still used as targets for darts. Fortunately, modern development has brought us a board with some form of permanency, if not in material at least in the playing 'face'.
This is the 'Standard' board. The reasons for the gradual emergence of today's board are lost in the hazy traditions of the sport. But its acceptance is one of the progressive moves of this sport and we can assume that the board most commonly used today is here to stay.
Cousins of the standard board still exist in the murky backwaters of the darts world. In the British Isles, where traditions are sacred and forged to last, cottage industries still produce small, black, round targets with no inner treble rings, minute center 'bulls' and impossible outer double rings, to hang on the walls of smoky taverns. To these traditional targets today's big, bright, colored board bears little resemblance, but provides no less of a challenge. Standardization has brought about the modern board. With teams travelling internationally to compete; with games played under a battery of television cameras for the entertainment of millions, and with sponsorship running into the millions of dollars, the sport has to present a familiar face to the public. Without standardization of equipment and rules. The popularity of the

game up to today's level just would not have been possible.

Major credit for promotion of the game should go to the 'News of the World', a major British newspaper, and to the National Darts Association of Great Britain for their contributions not only to creating an international forum for the sport but also to establishing basic acceptable rules of play. The formation of standard distances, equipment, and game rules should be the objective of every local and national organization.

Back to the board. All references in this book, therefore, take the 'clock', as shown on page (12), as the common board with its two center bull rings (single and double), an elusive treble ring, and an outer double ring.

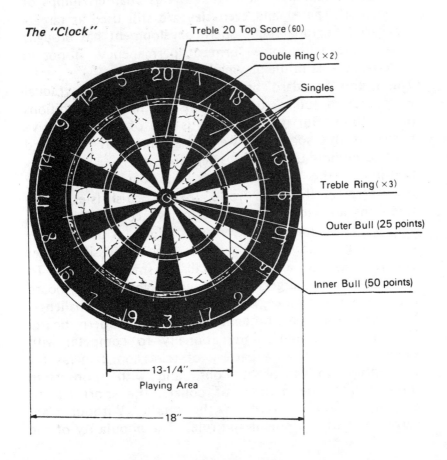

The "Clock"

Treble 20 Top Score (60)

Double Ring (×2)

Singles

Treble Ring (×3)

Outer Bull (25 points)

Inner Bull (50 points)

— 13-1/4" —

Playing Area

— 18" —

Some relatives of the 'clock' are described in the following pages. They cannot be overlooked, primarily because no modern book on the sport would be complete without them, but also because the areas of England where they are still used are major breeding grounds for some of the world's best players.

The board in most American darts centers is the standard type — 18" in diameter with a 13-1/4" playing area.

It has a double outer ring, a treble-value inner ring and a single/double bull. The numbers on the board rarely vary in position, they read as shown:

The actual playing area has the following dimensions:
* 6-5/8 inches from the center of the bull to the outer wire on the double.
* 6-1/4 inches from the center of the bull to the inner wire on the double.
* 4-1/8 inches from the center of the bull to the outer wire on the treble.
* 3-3/4 inches from the center of the bull to the inner wire on the treble.

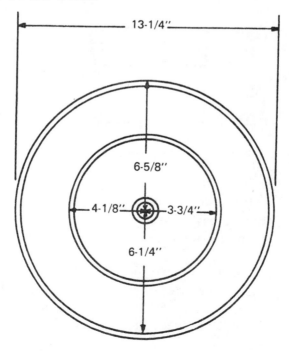

The doubles and trebles are, surprisingly, not as small as they appear from eight feet away. Take a look at the points of your darts and you'll see how much room there is for them in the double and treble sections. Illustrated below are their *actual sizes* with dimensions.

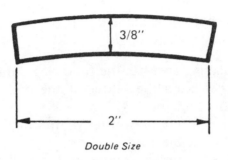

Double Size

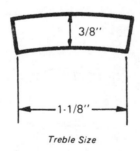

Treble Size

Curiously, these areas appear to get larger after a few beers and then progressively diminish as the evening wears on.

The bull may be the biggest surprise of all as the optical illusion of the concentric lines produces the effect of smallness, when actually it has more space than two double ring areas combined. Most proficient players find

14

the bull a relatively easy target, though for many beginners hitting one is an evening's achievement.
Below are its actual sizes.

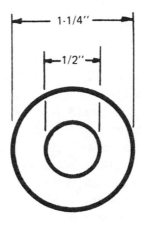

Bull Size

The thickness of the board varies but is important since it provides a cushioning effect. A dart landing in a thin board produces a loud unpleasant 'clonk', a good board a comfortable 'thud'. Apart from this, thickness has to be considered when measuring the distance to the throwing line, which will be discussed later.

The board which receives the most popularity among pubs and players alike is the 'Bristle'.

This is a heavy duty board with a thickness of 1-1/2 inches including a chipboard back frame. Some players claim it actually improves with play. The more darts it receives the more compressed its fibers become. It is good for many years of pounding and is tough to damage if mounted and treated properly.

The bristle board is made by a patented method using tufts of sisal, the fiber used for making ropes, into 'biscuits'. A 'biscuit' is a section of compressed sisal sliced off a long thick rope of fiber. The rope is wrapped with brown paper. After being chopped off like slices of salami the 'biscuits' are machine-packed to form the board at pressures exceeding 10 tons. All those wiggly lines you see on a new bristle board are the paper ends of each 'biscuit'. There are around fifty 'biscuits' per board. To assure the bristles don't grow mushrooms, and the like, the board is sprayed with a special fungicide. On these boards the darts do not leave their mark or chew holes as they do with other boards made of wood, cork or cardboard. As a matter of fact, the spider wires will tend to show the wear of the board long before the board itself does. This, however, can be easily corrected by changing the outside number ring and turning the board accordingly two spaces to insure even wear and tear. Some boards are available, at slightly higher prices, with special high grade steel strip being used for the rings and inlaid in the board. This strip is about five times thinner than the conventional wire giving much larger treble, double, and bull target areas. Also the dart has a better chance of sticking in the board and not bouncing out.

In addition, most bristle boards have non-fade colors that make the segments stand out for easy targeting.

The ultimate in dartboard sophistication is the hand-tooled board made of elm. This type of board is a primary choice for tournament play as well as a preferred standard for some pubs. The beauty of the wood and the way it receives darts are no small reasons for its popularity at top levels of darts play. Many good log-end elm boards have as many as 100 staples to hold the spider wires permanently secure.

They do however have their drawbacks as a pub fixture. Continual wear and tear from heavy blunt darts in the hands of ferocious chuckers (See Page 42. The Bomber) can shred them, and an inconsiderate owner can allow them to dry up and crack.

The elm board is a thoroughbred and demands treatment as such. Regular soaking in water or beer (preferably spillage from the taps) is imperative to prevent the wood from splitting.

This is one reason why the bristle board has become king, no soaking or any treatment is required. The only thing to remember with a bristle board is not to store it in an air-tight box, it needs breathing space, and to turn the number wire now and again. The board should be mounted solidly to prevent distortion. It is also worth remembering that hooked dart points will pull out fibers when removed from the board. So always keep sharp darts.

Cork is another material used for dartboards, experimented on for a number of years in the U.K. but now

"He's trying to make something called a 'bristle board"

with a nucleus of popularity in the U.S.A., though there are still some fine old pubs in England preserving cork boards. Cork really suffers under constant hammering. It cannot take the thumping of modern brass barrel darts, and when used by aficionados, special lightweight wooden darts, or French darts, are necessary to ensure some longevity of the board. As a regular pub fixture cork boards, though extremely pleasant and rewarding to play on, cannot be recommended.

The coiled paper board is an inexpensive buy for the beginner to stick up at home and practice on. Its life is limited as the paper rings distort with a lot of play and there is no firm anchorage for the spider staples. But by the time you have worn out your paper board you should be ready to graduate to a bristle type. The paper board is ideal for its market as it is an economical way of giving the game the exposure that can enhance its growth.

One of the most unbelievable dartboards ever was owned by a bearded fellow called Bill, a venerable inventor, who lived in a cave by the Pacific. Yes, in a cave! Inside the cave, a wooden house had been fitted and in this retreat, Bill hung his dartboard. It was no ordinary board, its only identifiable feature being that it was round. The face was like a relief map of Afganistan and where the bull should have been, there was a hole about the size of a quarter dollar. All wires had long since disappeared, corroded away by the wind blown brine of the Pacific. But one or two numbers were still recognizable.

Bill deeply loved a game of darts and would practice for hours on his "board" — sometimes, on fine days, taking it out onto his deck above the rocks and throwing under the sun. Once or twice a week, he'd go into town and persuade somebody, usually a stranger, to give him a game. The sad thing is, there's no known record of him ever having won a game. But for sheer devotion he couldn't be beaten.

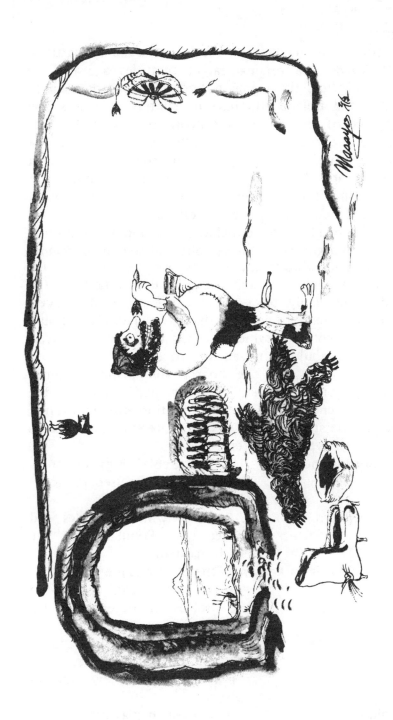

Colors

The colors on the face of the board are only partially standardized. The original target centuries ago had no colors to offset the segments and some boards used in England and Ireland still have no contrasting colors. The emergence of the multi-color board popular today was probably due to one of the earlier wood merchants with a bright idea and a pot of paint. The color patterns used nowadays are almost unlimited. The most common are the combinations of yellow/black, marble white/black with a red bull and marble white/black with a red outer bull and a black center bunghole. Also popular is alternating reds and greens on the doubles and trebles. Combinations of blue/white/black boards are produced though they're not such a familiar sight. The periphery of the island is invariably black to suit the mood of players whose darts tend to inhabit that area. The 20's should always be a colored segment. That's why, for even wear, the numbers should be moved two spaces.

Below are a few of the boards still being produced and played on in Britain. They are made to satisfy the demands of enclaves of die-hard traditionalists who refuse to accept the standard board. Others are specialists boards for particular types of contest.

The Yorkshire board: Has no treble rings or outer bull. Still widely used in North England.

The Irish Board: All black without trebles and outer bull. Popular with the Irish, naturally.

Burton board, (also known as the Staffordshire board):   An ancient board, again with no trebles or outer bulls. Instead of the outer bulls, two diamonds left and right, count for 25 points. Often called a "practice board" by veteran players.

Lincoln board: Has a 15-inch playing area. No trebles, no outer bulls.

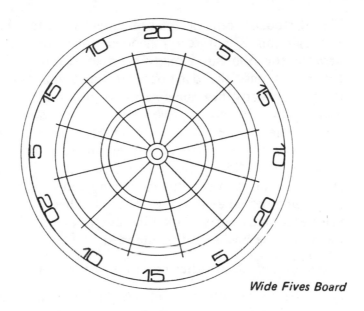

Wide Fives Board

The "wide fives" and "narrow fives" boards are basically the same, the "narrow fives" board having very thin doubles and trebles areas.

The log-end Manchester board, usually hand-made and still a favorite in Manchester and its environs is an extremely tough board to play, having a much smaller 10" playing area, no trebles and outer bull, and only matchstick-thin double rings. The board also has a black background, making segments almost impossible to see through the smoky fog usually found in Manchester pubs.

The boards are made of elm and need careful maintenance. Surprisingly, the Manchester board has a handful of fans in the U.S. and other countries, but is never likely to again achieve the popularity it once knew back home amidst the cotton mills of Lancashire.

> A unique world record has been established for hitting 1,000,001 on a Kent board. This is a small board with no trebles. A team of Kentishmen did it in 31 hours 43 minutes.

The dartboard can be placed directly onto the wall, although this is not recommended unless one lives in a barn or the pub has already been condemned. Even the best of us miss the dartboard at times and put one off the board. Many beginners seem to prefer to play on the wall around the board. Even though wild darts will not tumble the building they can make an unsightly mess, which is why most boards are hung on some kind of base. It should be solid but not too hard, as its function besides guarding your satin smooth mahogany veneer is to protect the point of the straying dart. A sheet of polished hammered brass may look nice but does not do the job for which the backboard is intended.

There are only four other criteria in hanging the board.

1) The center of the bull should be 5' 8" above the level of the hockey (throwing line).
2) The board face should be vertical.
3) The 20 segment should be at the top of the clock and straight.
4) The board should not swing or wobble.

It is amazing how often the critical 5' 8" height is overlooked. Good players know with a glance whether the board is too high or too low. A board in the wrong position is practically unplayable for the man with a well-tuned style and stance.

The important thing is that this 5' 8" be taken from the level of the hockey, not from the wall base. This means it is perfectly legal, though not very practical, if the hockey is in a hole and the board is raised an equivalent distance above floor level. Pubs with low ceilings have been known to make a trench for the players to stand in to get the board at the requisite height.

The board is often the pride of a pub and treated with as much love and affection as a pet chihuahua. Some pubs go to the worthwhile efforts of cutting an automobile tire in half and placing the board in its center. The tire is ideal for saving darts points and can be painted any color, carry a sponsor's advertisement, or the team's name.

Tire Enclosure

Landlords who like to 'put the game away', or lock up the board to prevent theft, enclose it in a cabinet with doors. Ready-made cabinets are on the market but it is easy to construct one to suit the bar decor. Some interesting ones are made of driftwood, bamboo, half a beer barrel, and an old leather suitcase.

The most useful thing about a spacious cabinet is that it can create a self-contained darts center, with accommodation for darts, chalk, wipers, scoreboard, spares, chewing gum, aspirins, etc.

Once the dartboard is in the cabinet a piece of plywood with an 18" hole cut in it is sometimes placed flush with the board face.

There are no set rules on the board surroundings, the main aim is to make an area conducive to good darts play and to the required specifications, but too many frills and fancy fixtures might distract the thrower.

Life Ring Enclosure

Cabinet Enclosure

24

> The electronic dart scoreboard used in the
> News of the World championships to relay
> scores to the audience was first introduced as
> early as 1938.

When marking off the distance to the hockey the thickness of the dartboard and its backboard should be taken into account, so the face of the board is taken as the starting point for the throwing distance.

NOTE:

The distance from the board to the hockey can and does vary in different localities. This is another traditional aspect of the sport that causes all sorts of headaches for national and international organizers.

In England, for example, the hockey distance changes by as much as three feet as one moves around the country. Some areas maintain a long nine feet line while in a few of the middle counties of England they throw from six feet. But whatever the established distance in your area, do not forget to allow those two or three inches of board thickness when measuring up for a throwing line. Eight feet can be considered the standard distance of play. The largest international contest in the world, the News of the World Championship has designated eight feet as the hockey position for Area, Divisional and Grand Final matches, but they allow local rules to prevail for preliminary matches.

The National Darts Association of Great Britain has made a smart move for their competitions by specifying seven feet six inches as the minimum distance, therefore allowing anybody to throw from as far back as he likes. All major American tournaments use 7 feet 9¼ inches as the standard distance.

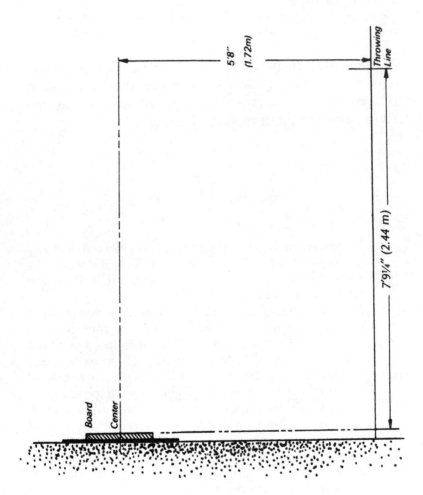

The Mat

In almost every pub in the British Isles and out of the British Isles one will see a mat stretched out from the board. It will have on it, in most cases, three throwing lines 8', 8' 6" and 9'. Compromising like this sells more mats and makes everybody happy. Prior to any match the teams should agree on the minimum throwing distance to avoid arguments and threats of disqualification later. The three line mat is often misunderstood. The eight foot line is not the ladies' line, the different distances have been put there merely to accommodate the big variations in local rules in England where most mats are made.

More than likely, the landlord or club manager rules the roost and will have his own pub or club laws on the hockey distance.

> From 1980 onwards only metric measurements will be used to specify distances in Britain. The hockey will be at a minimum of 2.28 meters (7'6") and the bull will be 1.74 meters from the ground. Also winning a game will earn 0.473 liters of beer and if you don't buy one for the winner you may be thrashed within 2.54 centimeters of your life.

The mat, by the way, apart from showing distances is a highly useful piece of equipment. It is usually made of corrugated rubber or plastic, extends ten feet from the board, and is about two feet wide. Each hockey is around eighteen inches long. In some top competitions the hockey is a raised block to make 100 percent sure throwers don't have wet feet (foot fault). The mat can save the floor from damage by rebounding darts, save the points of the darts, and save a carpet from having a track worn in it from the hooves of heavy players. The mat is also a favorite advertising medium, quite often for beer, cigarettes, dart equipment, or any other vices darts players are prone to.

In the absence of a mat a piece of tape can be stuck on the floor for a hockey, or, if you want it to be more permanent, a row of carpet tacks make a distinctive line.

The Scoreboard

A most essential fixture. There's nothing to beat the old-fashioned blackboard and chalk for a scoreboard. The new 'magic' boards for felt tip marking pens are okay but they're messy and it's almost impossible to avoid getting black fingers as many players like to wipe out numbers with a casual swipe of the hand.

If possible, the scoreboard should be attached to the left of the board so players marking up scores don't have to stand in the throwing area. There's no reason why the following player should wait while the other fellow hovers around the board trying to figure out his score, so a completely independent scoreboard attached out of the way is the best arrangement.

Besides recording game scores the board also serves to list the initials of waiting challengers, so should be a good size. In the cabinet layout the doors invariably have scoring areas inside. If there is room in the bar, a single door cabinet, opening to the left is better than two doors as this layout keeps the scorekeeper away from the playing area, and keeps all scores on one board.

> For millionaires there are electrical score-keepers that sell for over eight thousand dollars.

Lighting and General Aspects

Lighting is very important for good darts play although a seasoned player could probably pluck them off in a power cut. Playing by candlelight during the energy crisis hasn't seemed to dim the popularity or the actual playing of the game. Nor have there been any recorded injuries. The best lighting set-up is to have two spotlights, slightly overhead and to each side, angled in directly at the target.

Of course, the lights should have a back protecting cover to keep the light out of the thrower's eyes, and darts out of the light. Proper lighting should: 1) clearly illuminate all areas of the board and 2) provide that the least shadow area is created by a dart in the board.

To describe the perfect darts playing environment is next to impossible, it would be easier to describe the perfect wife. But once a player is married to a pub and a board it becomes for him the best place in the world to play.

Dart Equipment

As you can guess, the myriad types of darts around nowadays defy complete description. But a pointer or two to a few of the more popular types of arrows in use may be useful.

Although keen players may equip themselves with all kinds of paraphenalia from pocket calculators to finger powder, one of the beauties about the sport is that it can cost you next to nothing. Three arrows, a point at one end, flights at the other, and you have sufficient equipment to become a world champion.

One of the reasons why so many different types of darts are seen around is largely due to fetishes, fashions, and superstitions. Feathers come in all colors of the rainbow, and you sometimes even find them all on one dart, and barrels have as many different styles as the dart engineers can think of.

Weight is the most definitive factor of the dart. Regular production darts run from a lightweight 10 grams up to (and sometimes beyond) 40 gram blockbusters, with all weights in between usually available. The heaviest production brass dart in the world is a mighty 46 grams. Selection within this range depends entirely upon individual preference but generally speaking mid-range weights from 20 to 30 grams are the most popular.

Very light darts require much more thrust to get them to the board and this often upsets throwing balance and accuracy. Grip is the next important factor. A dart that just doesn't feel right just isn't going to travel right, so

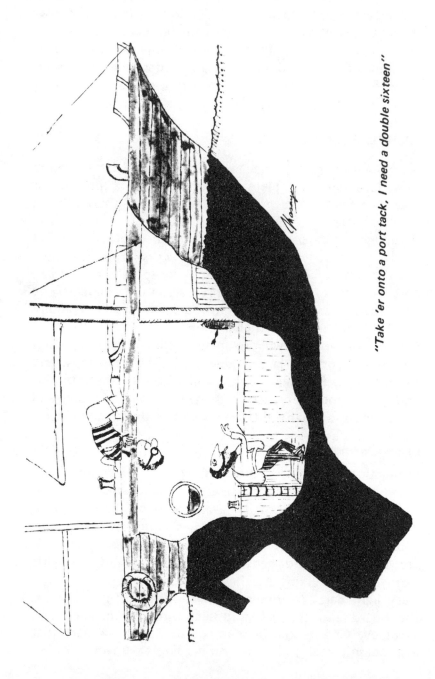

"Take 'er onto a port tack, I need a double sixteen"

when choosing your darts don't go by sight alone. Put them to a grip test. Many darts have little or no grip aid such as a knurled section or ridges. Satin-smooth surfaces and thin barrels are generally preferred by people with the dry slim hands and the sensitive touch of a concert pianist. If you're not a concert pianist and earn your living by hauling in cod nets then we suggest good heavy knurling on a fat barrel for a solid grip.

Throwers falling between these two categories have innumerable types to chose from. One major manufacturer produces over 100 patterns. Another important aspect is balance but as most darts are mass-produced nowadays they are pre-balanced thus the only factor to consider is whether the particular balance of the dart is suitable for your type of grip and throw.

The perfect dart, the one that will always find treble 20, has not yet been created so the best you can do is find a dart you enjoy throwing, feels natural, and can use with some competence.

Northern lumberjacks are playing darts with double bladed axes thrown into log's end. Spectators are advised to stand at least 50 yards away.

The French dart, those all-wooden-barrel-and-shaft beauties used a great deal in Philadelphia, are in much demand but hard to find. They are made of soft wood and have an H-shaped lead wrap-around weight inset in the barrel. Genuine French darts are produced amongst the mountains of Jura in France, but since this is a small cottage industry there is a constant shortage.

The bits of paper, feathers, plastic or what-have-you stuck on the ends of darts certainly affect flight paths. It is a matter of personal preference whether you have a flight tucked up against the barrel or at the end of a long stem. A popular style is the feathered flight that has the feathers running the whole length of a long shaft.

Thick plastic flights are best for 'house darts' that receive heavy punishment at the hands of every chucker who walks in the bar, but as a personal dart for the advanced player they cannot be recommended. Modern technology has brought us a new flight made of paper-thin polyvinyl film. These are flexible enough not to interfere too much with the passage of a following dart, and if a flight meets one already in the board the whole flight will pop off the stem, leaving the rest of the dart in the board.

"Any idea where I can get some of these new polly flights?"

Close grouping of darts is the aim of most throwers and in such a siutation a solid plastic flight will very often deflect a following dart, skidding it into some undesirable number. Some plastic flights are built onto a swivel so a dart hitting them will spin the flights out of the way. Feathered flights will part to allow the point of a passing arrow to cut through and allow tighter clustering. Split feathers can easily be reset with a sweep of the hand. The deflection problem also occurs with paper flights and in some cases a point will actually bury itself in the trailing edge of a thick paper flight. Most experts favor feathered flights or polyfilm flights.

A maestro at the game is Mr. Joseph Hitchcock of England. He takes on champions, and usually beats them, using only sharpened six inch nails. One of his favorite tricks is to knock a button from between outstretched fingers with his improvised darts.

Turkey feathers are the best in the world for a set of flights. Unfortunately this is another raw material that is getting increasingly hard to find. The feathers best for a dart come from the leading edge of the wings. This is where the feathers grow strong and rigid, but only a couple of darts can be outfitted from one turkey. With

modern battery breeding methods the turkeys never get off the ground, so to speak, and turkey wings don't get the chance to develop and strengthen. There's also less demand for the hefty 30 pounders than there used to be, making the perfect feathered bird hard to find nowadays. Mechanical plucking of turkeys should be banned as it chews up most featheres. To ensure a constant supply of top class flights the best thing is for the keen player to breed his own turkeys — the old grey mottled bird has the best feathers and it should be allowed to grow to at least above 25 pounds and taught low altitude flying early in life, perhaps on a leash in the yard, so its feathers grow strong and healthy.

A rather unusual design of flight is a synthetic fiber type designed to let a dart cut through like the feathered flights. It looks very much like a bottle washer. This type is best used in lighter darts as it doesn't provide quite as much lift as regular flights.

The barrel of the dart is the bit between the point and the shaft, though some arrows, including those nice old wooden jobs are all one piece. Modern barrels are made out of all manner of material. The News of the World presents solid silver arrows as part of its championship series; not the kind to leave lying around on some strange bar. Gold plated darts are a standard catalogue item of one major manufacturer. Brass is the most used metal for barrels. Steel is sometimes used for cheaper types but tends to rust with regular exposure to beer. Heavy tungsten alloy is an excellent alternative to brass, heavy and durable, and a lot more expensive.

And the latest heavy metal to be used is nickel silver. The objective in using these expensive metals is to maintain weight while slimming down the barrel. A heavy dart of tungsten for example is about one-third the thickness of a regular brass dart.

Chrome plated grips are common but are often too slippery for people with perspiring paws. Slim barrels and barrels with noses that are not blunt find their way more easily through arrows already in the board and should be the choice of the good grouper.

Many experts attach great importance to the stem, working on the principle the thinner the better. With a cane stem you can shave it down until it is no thicker than a toothpick, but you can't expect it to withstand rough use. Fiber glass and alloy are also used for the stem as lightness is the main objective, the stem and flight only giving balance and stability to the dart during its journey to the board.

A case for darts.

Get a case. If your darts don't come in one (most do) when you buy them, then make one out of an old cigar box (sticking an eraser inside to hold the points) or anything that will stop your flights from breaking or getting ruffled. On the market are some fine leather cases and darts purses to slip into a pocket. You can even get them today with your name in gilt.

Other accessories, (the value of some is questionable,) include finger grip wax and pocket-size score calculators if you're not so hot on mental math. Having the ability to know immediately where your next dart should go is far better than having to fumble in your pocket for a calculator.

A really valuable little item to include in your darts case is a sharpener. These are handy little silicon carbide stones much like a snooker cue chalk and should be used regularly. A blunt dart doesn't do the board any good and can all too easily bounce off a wire, rather than slide around it.

Spares

Persuade your friendly local tavern owner to keep a good stock of spare flights behind the bar. If he isn't so friendly then keep a few spares at home.

It is another sad fact of life that the best flights are the ones that get damaged most easily. Also, the better you are the closer you will group the darts and the faster you'll slice away a nice set of flights. Top class players have been known to change their flights after every game.

The barrels aren't so prone to punishment. A set of brass barrels will serve for many years and with regular use develop a lovely mellow look. Snuggling a familiar, well-worn barrel between your fingers can be equal to starting the game a leg up. With modern standardized adapters the spare flights available will fit into almost any barrel. Alloy tipped adapters are superior to plastic as they will not split if the point of a dart finds its way inside. Obtaining paper flights poses no problems if you favor that type of dart. And trying to fold one of the ready-cut sets without previous experience can provide hours of fun.

CHAPTER III

The Do's and Don'ts of Dart Throwing

Stance

It is no use trying to tell a veteran darts player that he throws and stands all wrong. The most it can earn is an angry glare and perhaps a challenge to prove whose stance is better. But like most precision sports, a bad form may serve the player well for years and years but he will no doubt wonder why he can never climb above a certain level of competence. And as with any other sports, there are always the few exceptions to the rule. So, although the following may bring snorts of — "Well, how about good old Hairy Harry? He throws balanced on one toe", — it can generally be accepted that the majority of truly great dart players stick to the basic laws because they have been proven to result in a more accurate throw.

The major thing about the stance is that both feet should be flat and firm on the mat. Certainly the easiest and best position is toes to the hockey and feet slightly apart.

This is the way Tom Barret, one of the best darts players of all time, and dozens of other champions throw. It means you are well-balanced at all times with about 60% of your weight on your right foot and you have full face to the board so that your focus angle is square.

Many players find it more comfortable to open the foot opposite to the hand they use, and there's no real harm done as long as the feet remain planted. The more you move the left foot the more weight you'll be shifting onto the right foot.

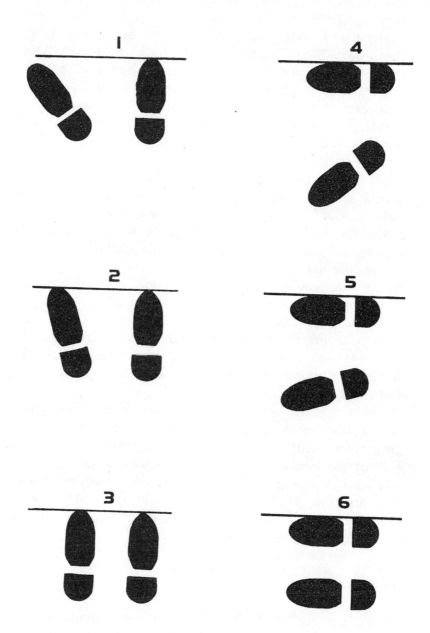

Remember, you have two eyes so you may as well use them both to best advantage. As an interesting experiment, try throwing with only one eye open. You'll find that you will have to adjust your throw drastically. Then try it with the other eye. The same applies to a lesser degree when the head is twisted and your left eye has to peer over the bridge of your nose. So if you are a beginner, or even if you are not, face the board, stand upright solidly planted on both feet with both eyes glued straight on the target. And relax.

There should be very little body movement. Swaying kills accuracy and makes your darts inconsistent. A good balance and repetitive arm action are what you should strive for and practice. No bending of the knees, no bowing forward like a praying mantis and no cute little lifts of the heels.

Sure, you may have seen some good players twisting, turning and prancing all over the place like a wounded octopus. They have a sway and an individual style that they have practiced for years and years — but they still have to make adjustments for every dart they throw. So leave the swaying to the golfers, and don't start off with bad habits.

Another point to watch is that when you've finished your throw, you should be in exactly the same position, apart from your arm, as when you started. Jumping from one side of the hockey to the other is frowned upon in most circles, but a slight shuffling to position yourself better for squeezing in that last treble 20 is okay. Standing to either side of the hockey also lengthens the distance to the board, which isn't a good idea.

The Throw

Ideally towards the board. This not only tends to win more games but it also cuts down on injuries. Seriously, the throw is naturally the most important aspect of the darts movement. As already stated, the only thing to move should be your arm.

The Bomber

The winner of the 1950 News of the World Championship was a 6'5" metal worker who was a rapid. fire artist, taking an average of only four seconds for each throw.

Again, the best style is the one used by the majority of the experts. At the same time, each throw is like a signature and no two throws are exactly alike. The arm is at a right angle to the body, the hand tucked back with the dart alongside the eye on the line of flight. Relax the wrist and then move it fast from the elbow. The dart should be shoved on its way so that it travels fast and as flat as possible. It should not be allowed to glide in a slow curve through the air. The lob at darts is usually the sign of a mediocre player. The expert only uses the lob to put his darts up and over another dart that may be blocking his target. The movement of the arm with a full smooth follow-through with fingers, thumb, and the dart pointing directly at the targeted area completes the perfectly executed style.

Follow-through is absolutely essential, and the forearm should finish up extended toward the board at about a 30° angle. Make sure the fingers and thumb are pointing at the target at the time of release, as though you're pointing a finger of accusation. The fingers and thumb are the last guiding force in the final destination of the dart.

The speed of a dart hitting the board is around 40 mph.

Remember the 4-Fs: *firm, fast, flat, follow* — Practice this way and your potential for improvement is unlimited.
If the dart wobbles on its way to the board like a sick sparrow, then there is either something very wrong with the dart or your grip needs changing.

The Ballerina

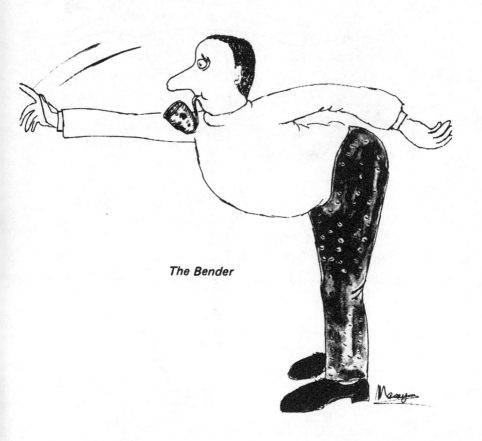

The Bender

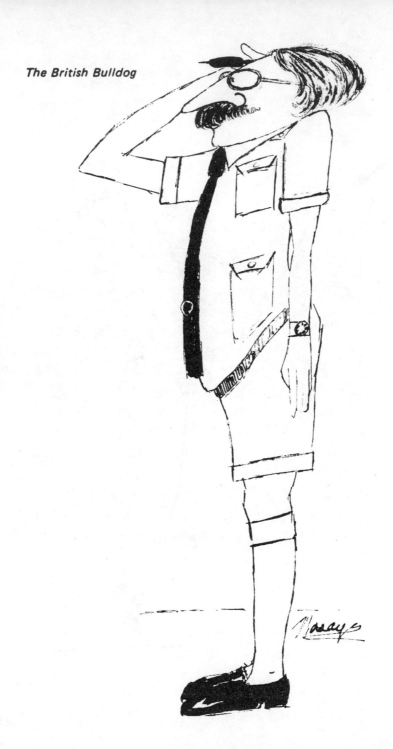

The British Bulldog

Big Chief Wetfoot

The Beautician

The Beginner

The Grip

The type of grip you use depends to a great extent on the type of darts you favor and vice-versa. If you've sorted that out, then let's explain a little further. Nearly all, if not all, modern metal barrel darts come with a knurled or serrated section to provide a non-slip grip. The length of this grip area should be considered as to whether you will use a two, three, four or even a five fingered grip. (Each finger firmly planted on or around the dart's center of balance) To illustrate this, here are two extremes:

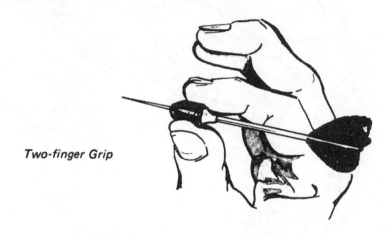

Two-finger Grip

Five-finger Grip

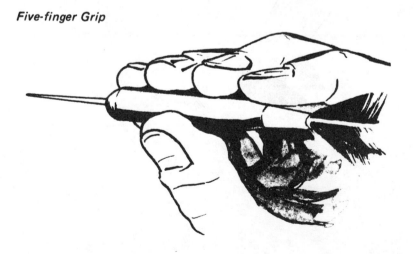

The Best

Both of the grips shown here are unusual and not particularly recommended; two fingers giving very little directional control and five fingers giving too much top heavy control.

The best type of grips are with three or four fingers. Experts favor a four-finger hold with two above the dart and two below. This is an excellent balanced grip and seems to work well enough for the champions.

A popular and simple grip is the 'pen holder'. The thumb and index finger are on either side of the balance point and the middle finger acts as support at the front of the dart for better control. To change this to a four-finger grip is easy enough as the middle finger is moved up and placed on top, the thumb is still the balance point and the third finger acts as a forward controller, almost under the needle of the dart. This latter four-finger job is certainly an expert's grip and it takes a lot of practice to get used to. Unless the dart is held and pushed at the right place, it will corkscrew to the board like a spent rocket and probably end up on the floor. Whether changing the grip to give an angled lob or to deflect the flight upward is open to debate and certainly shouldn't be used in contest without a lot of intensive practice.

Finger grip wax is now obtainable in scented tablets. Cologne is the only scent now available.

The grip that is most comfortable and familiar is probably the best one, and without a lot of practice a new grip would undoubtedly hurt your game — especially if you try to change in mid-career. For beginners, we strongly recommend starting with the four-finger grip as sketched below if your ambitions include reaching the pinnacles of the darts world.

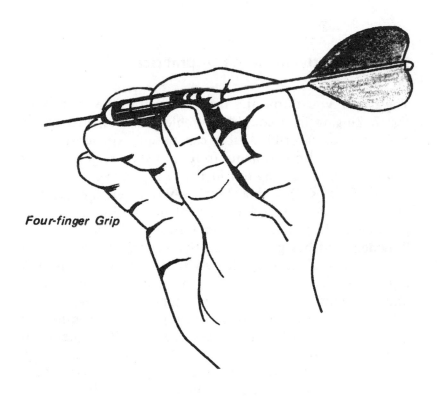

Four-finger Grip

Another factor — one which doesn't have a great deal of bearing on the subject — is the size of the hand. It is logical that a fellow with paws like a grizzly shouldn't adopt a four-finger grip when he favors toothpick-size darts. And delving deeper into this reservoir of common sense, it also goes that a little old lady with spidery fingers shouldn't attempt to throw 45 megaton lumberjack's darts with a dainty two finger grip.

CHAPTER IV

Practice makes perfect

How to get the most out of practice.

The better you throw the more enjoyable the game gets, right? Zinging in a couple of treble twenties, then going out on your favorite double can be an experience equal to holing out from a ninety-foot chip shot at golf, hitting a home run, or striking out in the tenth frame.

So, it follows that the best way to get the greatest number of such experiences out of this skillful game is to practice, and practice for at least an hour every day.

Provided God has granted you five fingers at the end of a reasonably straight arm, plus a vision that extends at least eight feet, we can promise that you'll see impressive improvements in your game after a few months of following an organized hour-a-day practice schedule. To get the most value out of these sessions it is important that you follow a set practice pattern, even keep a record, so you can not only chart your progress but also make practice more interesting. An hour's aimless throwing at the board doesn't help develop a keenly honed movement and can get pretty boring.

Concentrate also on synchronizing your style, even to the extent of counting to yourself, much like practicing a dance step. In time this will give you a steady pace of throw. Pace is an often overlooked aspect of the game, but a player with a natural relaxed pace can often get the edge over an opponent who gets flustered and erratic in a tight spot.

The late Jim Pike, a darts legend in England, was such a marksman that he could shoot a cigarette from a bystander's mouth with a dart and impale it in any named double.

If you are a beginner, we suggest you start off by trying to group your darts. Simply throw one anywhere in the board and attempt to make the following two hug it as closely as possible. As an aid in this approach, cut out circles of paper or cardboard in diminishing sizes starting with about a four inch diameter and ending with an inch diameter. When you succeed in placing all three darts into the circle, replace the circle with the next smaller size and so on. Also move the circles to different parts of the board.

When some degree of consistency is achieved in your grouping, start moving around the clock hitting each number from 1 to 20. Keep a check on the number of darts the full round takes, but forget about the time element. Don't rush. Remember pace. Accuracy is more critical than speed (unless you want to break world records) and rushing between the board and the hockey will only leave you a panting wreck with no improvement in your game.

Once you've become reasonably proficient at whizzing round the clock — ideally in twenty darts but practically, we suggest in around forty, try the same thing on doubles. A good round would be about 60 darts.

London, 1937. The late and great Jim Pike went round the board on doubles, retrieving his own darts, in the time of 3 minutes 30 seconds.

Many players have a favorite double, which is a good idea until they miss it, then they find themselves floundering around the board until they eventually end up on double 1's, in the meantime allowing their opponents to catch up on score and steal the game. Having only one double up your sleeve is very often the easiest way to snatch defeat from the jaws of victory. Being capable on all the doubles is the healthiest way to ensure you won't be left on an unfavourable number, and it allows you to go out by the quickest route possible.

So plenty of round-the-clock practice on singles and doubles, and you'll soon be winning prizes.

Again, record your progress. Go round on doubles once every practice session. It is easy to make a wall chart to pin up by the board and keeping it up-to-date is an added incentive to stick to your hour-a-day schedule.

Add a few standard games of 301, 501 or 801 to your practice program and match yourself against par scores (see page 58), for example, finishing 301 in 21 darts can win most singles contests among average players.

If you keep company with players who earn money from the board, then you'd better aim for averaging around 12 darts.

Keep in mind that you tend to throw with more consistency when out of the normal game enviroment; there's no hanging around waiting for your opponent, no pressure and no distractions when you practice at home. Therefore don't try and establish your standard by your practice scores, this could lead to your over-estimating yourself and ending up buying a lot of drinks.

Can you score 101 in three darts by hitting three trebles? *

Familiarity with the standard game should also give you a better idea of finishing combinations so there's no need to break your throwing rhythm by standing at the hockey biting your finger nails while figuring which numbers to hit.

Don't forget the bull. Starting and finishing the standard game with a bull at either end is tough and if you can do it (301) in less than 15 darts you're getting good. Aiming arrow after arrow at the bull is not particularly good practice as your throw gets into a groove, so although you may find yourself hitting plenty of centers it doesn't really reflect your ability to hit one during the normal course of a game where you may only have one chance at it.

Introducing the bull frequently into the games you practice is a surer way of becoming a bull artist. The single bull circle is twice as large a target as any of the doubles, so isn't as tough as it appears.

* *No way*

Some fun ways to practice:

To inject a bit of amusement into practice hours, and at the same time to make yourself a more versatile player try these other forms of darts solitaire.

1. **Fifty-ones**

   For beginners. See how many times out of ten you can score fifty-one with three darts.

   Sounds easy? Treble 17 will give it to you with one throw, so will single 16, 17, 18. But there's more to it than you imagine.

   Par for ten tries: Beginners   — 2
                  Average   — 4
                  Expert   — 8

2. **Accumulation**

   For everybody, even a favorite challenge of the champs. With fifteen darts, (only three per throw, mind) go for the highest possible score. No cheating.

   Par score: Beginners   — 240
               Average   — 300
               Expert   — 400

   NOTE: *In a recent 15-dart contest in England, the following scores were recorded by the top three contestents.*

   > *Match yourself against the champs:*
   > *First Place   :   402 points*
   > *Second Place: 384 Points*
   > *Third Place   :   341 points*
   > *Or in another contest using only seven darts:*
   > *First Place   :   250 points*
   > *Second Place: 240 points*
   > *Third Place   :   203 points*
   > *Par score for seven darts: Beginners   — 150*
   > *   Average   — 200*
   > *Make a chart by playing 10 rounds each practice session. Keep the total score for each round and at the end of the 10 rounds add all together and divide by 10. This will give you the average for the evening. Mark the average on the chart. If this average goes progressively downwards try taking up tiddlywinks or bridge.*

Fifteen-darts accumulation

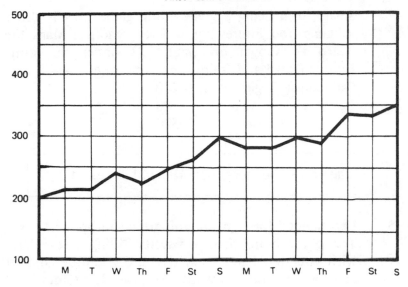

2-week chart

3. All Blacks

For beginners to average players. Put a dart in each of the black numbers starting with the lowest number and then go around the board clockwise. Give yourself one point for each hit and subtract a point for each miss. Remember only one dart per section (Total ten sections).

Par score: Beginners — 0
           Average — 4
           Expert — 8

Now try it on doubles. And if you feel ambitious — trebles.

4.   15 to Bull
      Apart from being a great group game, this is also a
      valuable and interesting way to practice. Mark the
      board as shown on page 121 under the game
      Double-Down and follow the same rules.
      Par scores: Beginner   — 200
                  Average   — 300
                  Expert   — 500

Can you score more than 180 with three darts? *

---

5.   Left-handed (or right, if you are a southpaw).
      Try it for more than a novelty. Fling a few darts
      with your left hand every day and you'll be amazed
      at what that normally idle paw can do besides hold
      a drink. You can keep this as your secret weapon
      and if you move in certain circles it could be a
      money-winner. The main principle is to duplicate as
      closely as possible the actions of your regular
      throwing hand, obeying the same grip, stance and
      throwing rules.
The primary objective of this chapter is to help you get
the most out of practicing. If you let practice become
tedious you'll do a lot less of it and there will always be
that fine edge of brilliance lacking in your contest games.
Practice has another important value. It gives you self-
confidence. Raw beginners have been known to buy
themselves a board, stick it up at home and practice
behind locked doors for weeks.
On emerging they've swaggered down to the local dartboard and whitewashed the fellow who kicked sand in
their faces a few weeks ago. Positive thinking has helped
many a neophyte win their games, and many a drink.
Let's explore this positive thinking angle a bit deeper. The
principle rule is to think not of what is going to happen
if you miss but where you are going when you hit. If you
*Turn 16 to the top of the board and it becomes 91. Three Trebles
give you 819.

do miss don't cast you next dart through a cloud of gloom, concentrate harder and slightly slow down your pace to make sure you don't miss a second time. Don't follow up a bad dart quickly — you will only end up with two bad darts. Many players miss badly and think by hurriedly hitting the target with the next dart they can quickly obliterate their mistake and save face in the eyes of their opponent. It seldom works.

Rid yourself of mental tension before stepping up to the hockey. Gallons of beer don't do this (though a few pints may help) since relaxation only comes with confidence in your own abilities. So move up to the hockey with the idea not necessarily that you are about to thrash an opponent, but that you are about to play your best game ever.

Some players retrieve their darts from the board like a raging bull after a bad throw while punishing walls with kicks and karate chops. If you are ever lucky enough to be matched against one of these in a competition, a calm confident you will likely carry the day.

A pub in Australia is the home of a particularly fiery group of players who regularly demolish the pub fixtures when the pressure is on, to counter their ferocity the landlord has installed at ground level under the board a big heavy canvas bag packed with beach sand. On the bag is printed an internationally famous four-letter expletive. This is a frustation bag, so nowadays instead of kicking down his walls, the pent up players land a heavy boot into the bag to let off steam. The right mixture of patience, mental discipline and physical control is the formula for winning darts. Any true champion at first eliminates his mental errors.

Mental practice & your opponent

However, practicing alone will always lack the one vital element your are bound to meet in a real game: the opponent. As he will undoubtedly have a great deal of influence on the final result of the game, your rival needs some consideration.

The best way to treat an opponent, after you have shaken hands and exchanged the usual cheerful pleasantries, is to ignore him. Apart from murmuring the occasional "Nice arrows" between your clenched teeth, play your own game and compete against yourself. You should know what score or how many darts your best-self can come up with so try and play to beat your top record.

But, since it is simply not human to be able to ignore your opponent completely, what shall we do about him? First of all, completely disregard his personal appearance. Physical attributes are of little help in this sport. A finely tuned athlete rippling his muscles on the hockey has no more advantage than an asthmatic clerk with terminal dandruff.

It is the positive thinker who starts with the big advantage. That does not mean thinking negatively about your opponent; you cannot expect to ride to victory on his mistakes.

Secondly, no matter how fast your opponent leaps around twix hockey and board don't be hustled into speeding up from your own regular pace.

As a summary to the chapter on practice here are a few tips:

* Seek new challenges next time you compete with other players. Don't look for the easy marks.
* Always play your own game, not their's.
* If you throw a bad miss, slow down for the next dart.
* Don't fool with your throws when playing against opponents not as skilled as yourself.
* Warm up with some practice before any game.

CHAPTER V

The standard game

For the avid player there is only one way to play darts — the standard game, 301, 501, 1001, ad infinitum. In the last chapter we talked about the mental aspects of the game. Although it may seem a lot of amateurish woffle to some, anybody who has competed at the standard game for a number of years will have discovered for himself that nights of aggravating mediocrity and nights of awe inspiring brilliance are separated only by a thin mental membrane.

Many game variations generously allow a large percentage of bad darts to be thrown without their influencing the final result too tragically. These games absorb mistakes. The standard game does· not. This is the game that elects champions. It is beautifully simple yet wickedly frustrating. Let's explain it very briefly:

The object is simple. You are given 301 (501 or 801, etc.) points, and all you have to do is get rid of them. There are, of course a couple of rules to complicate things. To start getting rid of this figure you have to first hit a double. And to polish off the 301 you must hit another double. But in between — anything goes.

The history of internationally competitive darts has been dominated by this game, so there's a lot more to it than meets the eye of the layman.

> In the News Of the Worlds Championship finals only two players have ever hit the golden 180, in 1966 and 1970.

In Britain over eight million fans hang over the tube watching the international champions aiming for the elusive 501 figure every year. Nine darts will give the score to anybody and there are numerous ways of closing out the number in these few darts. Only a handful of men in the world have the ability to make the nine-dart close-out a potential threat.

Under the pressure of international or national contests the authors have found only one player (John Lowe — See Chapter X) able to finish the game of 501 in nine darts.

This is interesting because it bears out the fact that mental pressure has an enormous effect. The same players who can impale a matchstick dangling from trembling lips, decapitate mosquitoes from eight feet and perform incredible feats of accuracy in exhibition games can flounder to a dismal 20 dart finish when placed under the tournament spotlights with a mere 501 to clean up.

The starting block for the standard game is a double, any double on the board. Once a double has been hit all that's necessary is the fastest streak possible down the stretch until the finishing line — another double. Trying to get that first double can lead to insanity.

Strong men have collapsed with frustration at the hockey because the great fat double they have religiously practiced to hit with at least two out of three darts suddenly becomes a Cleopatra's needle.

Mentally magnifying the double can help you get over the first hurdle.

Once the double score is safely registered, any dart landing in a number gets you closer to home. A treble 20 is most useful, three treble twenties are ecstasy. But beware, while hitting 20's in a bundle is fun, slightly missing 20's lands you in the rough; the 5's and 1's guard either side of the plum.

Downstairs, at the bottom of the board, remember we have the 19's, and this area is the target of players (very often, short players) who don't have any particular attraction for the tops. It is worth remembering that hitting a single 19 and closely missing with a 7 and a 3 (29) will leave you with more score for the throw than an equally bad throw upstairs (26).

Archimedes or some other mathematician must have worked out the number placement on the dartboard. Despite the fact that most people make a fetish out of the 20's, unless you can consistently hit three of them they have no more value than the 19's. Strange? Compare; 20 + 20 + 5 (miss-shot) = 45. 19 + 19 + 7 (mis-shot) = 45. 20 + 20 + 1 (miss-shot) = 41. 19 + 19 + 3 (mis-shot) = 41. Even if you're a very good average player, there's no reason not to adopt downstairs as your playground. If your opponent is scoring numbers like 85 with four 20's and a 5, your four 19's and a 7 only drops you two points behind him.

Upstairs or downstairs your basic objectives are the same, to score the most points to get you the fastest to that final double.

Strategy

Now we have hammered away at the big scores and brought down that 501 to a respectable size, we can start setting our sights on finishing off with a double. To do this you may take any of about a million tracks (subject to computer confirmation), but light is first seen at the end of the tunnel once you have reached the score of 170. At this score a couple of quick treble 20's and the last dart slipped smartly into the double bull will give you the game. Failing this, your next possible exit is attainable from a score of 167 (3 × 20, 3 × 19, bull) if you are a versatile player, and for the downstairs specialist two treble 19's and double bull with get rid of 164.

Closing possibilities for the realistic average player usually start at figures from below 100, though it should always be kept in mind that once past 170 victory may be only three darts away for you, and also for your opponent of course. Never discount the possibilities of a miracle finish.

A Mr. Douglas Priestner, warming up for a match, scored five consecutive 180's. It is not reported as to whether he won the match.

65

Beginners at the game have a natural inclination, due to the design of the board, to believe that the bull is the prime target whereas, in actual fact, its value comes very low down the scale when it comes to accumulation of score in the standard game. Three double bulls, a remarkable feat of accuracy, will produce the paltry score of 150 against three treble 20's, a wider target, which will produce 180. And any three trebles of 19, 18 or 17 scores more than the three double bulls. Openings or finishes on bull can safely be disregarded by all save the experts in the standard game.

Compare:

TWENTIES X 3	180	
NINETEENS X 3	171	
EIGHTEEEN X 3	162	
SEVENTEENS X 3	153	
BULLS X 3	150	

The following chart, laboriously compiled and the cause of numerous headaches and arguments between the authors could be of unending value to the reader. It may be quoted, photocopied or used by anybody at all without official permission. The authors also refuse to acknowledge any mistakes.

	1ST DART	2ND DART	3RD DART
170	3 x 20	3 x 20	BULL
169	NOT POSSIBLE		
168	NOT POSSIBLE		
167	3 x 20	3 x 19	BULL
166	NOT POSSIBLE		
165	NOT POSSIBLE		
164	3 x 19	3 x 19	BULL
163	NOT POSSIBLE		
162	NOT POSSIBLE		
161	3 x 20	3 x 17	BULL
160	3 x 20	3 x 20	2 x 20
159	NOT POSSIBLE		
158	3 x 20	3 x 20	2 x 19
157	3 x 20	3 x 19	2 x 20
156	3 x 20	3 x 20	2 x 18
155	3 x 20	3 x 19	2 x 19
154	3 x 20	3 x 18	2 x 20
153	3 x 20	3 x 19	2 x 18
152	3 x 20	3 x 20	2 x 16
151	3 x 20	3 x 17	2 x 20
150	3 x 20	BULL	2 x 20
149	3 x 20	3 x 19	2 x 16
148	3 x 20	3 x 16	2 x 20

147	3 x 20	3 x 17	2 x 18
146	3 x 20	3 x 18	2 x 16
145	3 x 20	3 x 15	2 x 20
144	3 x 20	3 x 18	2 x 15
143	3 x 20	3 x 17	2 x 16
142	3 x 20	BULL	2 x 16
141	3 x 20	3 x 17	2 x 15
140	3 x 20	3 x 20	2 x 10
139	3 x 20	3 x 19	2 x 11
138	3 x 20	3 x 18	2 x 12
137	3 x 20	3 x 19	2 x 10
136	3 x 20	3 x 20	2 x 8
135	3 x 20	3 x 15	2 x 15
134	3 x 20	3 x 18	2 x 10
133	3 x 20	3 x 11	2 x 20
132	3 x 20	3 x 12	2 x 18
131	3 x 20	3 x 17	2 x 10
130	3 x 20	3 x 10	2 x 20
129	3 x 20	3 x 13	2 x 15
128	3 x 20	3 x 16	2 x 10
127	3 x 19	3 x 10	2 x 20
126	3 x 20	3 x 12	2 x 15
125	3 x 20	3 x 15	2 x 10
124	3 x 20	3 x 12	2 x 14
123	3 x 20	3 x 13	2 x 12
122	3 x 20	3 x 10	2 x 16
121	3 x 20	3 x 7	2 x 20
120	3 x 20	20	2 x 20
119	3 x 20	19	2 x 20
118	3 x 20	18	2 x 20
117	3 x 20	17	2 x 20
116	3 x 20	16	2 x 20
115	3 x 20	15	2 x 20
114	3 x 20	14	2 x 20
113	3 x 20	13	2 x 20
112	3 x 20	12	2 x 20
111	3 x 20	11	2 x 20
110	3 x 20	BULL	
109	3 x 20	9	2 x 20
108	3 x 20	8	2 x 20
107	3 x 20	7	2 x 20
106	3 x 20	6	2 x 20
105	3 x 20	5	2 x 20
104	3 x 20	4	2 x 20
103	3 x 20	3	2 x 20
102	3 x 20	2	2 x 20
101	3 x 20	1	2 x 20
100	3 x 20	2 x 20	
99	3 x 19	10	2 x 16
98	3 x 20	2 x 19	
97	3 x 19	2 x 20	
96	3 x 20	2 x 18	
95	3 x 19	2 x 19	
94	3 x 18	2 x 20	
93	3 x 19	2 x 18	

92	3 x 20	2 x 16
91	3 x 17	2 x 20
90	3 x 20	2 x 15
89	3 x 19	2 x 16
88	3 x 16	2 x 20
87	3 x 17	2 x 18
86	3 x 18	2 x 16
85	3 x 15	2 x 20
84	3 x 18	2 x 15
83	3 x 17	2 x 16
82	3 x 14	2 x 20
81	3 x 17	2 x 15
80	3 x 16	2 x 16
79	3 x 13	2 x 20
78	3 x 16	2 x 15
77	3 x 19	2 x 10
76	3 x 20	2 x 8
75	3 x 15	2 x 15
74	3 x 14	2 x 16
73	3 x 19	2 x 8
72	3 x 12	2 x 18
71	3 x 17	2 x 10
70	3 x 10	2 x 20
69	3 x 13	2 x 15
68	3 x 16	2 x 10
67	3 x 17	2 x 8
66	3 x 12	2 x 15
65	3 x 15	2 x 10
64	3 x 16	2 x 8
63	3 x 11	2 x 15
62	3 x 10	2 x 16
61	3 x 7	2 x 20
60	20	2 x 20

The above chart, as mentioned, is not the answer-all for all darts players. As a matter of fact, many players might disagree with some of the suggested close-outs. Fine! to each his own. But a closer look at the doubles will show that over 70 percent of the close-outs are aimed at the 20's, 10's and the 16's, 8's. These are the areas that we recommend players should strive for.

Due to the unbelievable complexities of mathematics we have not made the chart cover every possibility. Naturally those numbers below 60 have been omitted as the logical finish should be apparent, and also because of the inumerable combinations available.

Despite the fact that in the section on practice we advocate versatility rather than favoritism on the doubles, in the standard game 20's and 16's are the usual choice of most players, versatility merely gives you a second line of defense.

Why the 16's? This is a buffer number. Missing double 16 can land you either in a single (leaving you on a double 8) or in double 8 (leaving you to repeat it) or in a single 8 (for a double 12 finish). Obviously, double top, apart from being the largest scoring double, (except double bull), is in the most popular area of the board and is a close friend of the competition player. It is for this reason we have used the double tops and 16's as close-out recommendation. Most good players will agree with our choice. Keep in mind that many of the close-outs shown are not the fastest route to victory — but they are the safest. When one is left with a hundred or less, it may be wise to play safe and use all three darts for a close-out rather than jeopardize a chance to end the game in that throw by trying for a two-dart finish. Numbers down from sixty are safe two dart finishes, with forty-eight the favorite launching pad for a game shot. Other two-dart combinations are so numerous with numbers from sixty they cannot all be listed. One interesting one, if you are left with a twenty-six there are just twenty-six ways to finish in two darts.

It is not always possible to leave yourself with a double 16 or 20 finish and you can safely assume that if you are not a top class player your first or second darts are going to be off target a good percentage of the time. To prepare yourself for mis-shots, memorize the alternative combinations so you have no worries no matter what score the first dart leaves you with.

Learning to accommodate these mis-shots can give you added confidence and not upset your playing rhythm; you merely make a slight adjustment.

It is highly useful to have a few of these winning combinations up your sleeve, top players rarely falter in their throw because they don't know where to put the next dart. Just learn a few of these finishes to start with and you'll be surprised at how quickly you'll be able to master most of the other possibilities.

Any number from 100 down (with the exception of 99) can be obtained with just two darts.

69

Game Rules

Bust

Any dart overscoring brings that throw to an abrupt halt. With say, twenty-five to go you hit a 19, then in going for double 3 you hit a 17, your throw is bust and you revert back to the twenty-five score. A little tip here, it is considered bad darts manners to hurl your third dart into the board in a fit of pique after you have already gone bust.

Busting is also accomplished should you equal the number you want, like going for a game shot of double 8 and hitting a single 16 by mistake — only a double ends the game.

A note of warning is also in order here. Once you have hit your intended double — that's it. Don't under any circumstance heave a triumphal last dart towards the board as it will very likely earn a cry of "Bust" from the scorer. Maybe this rule is not so strict in local friendly matches but if you make it a personal habit to hang fire once you have hit the double — it may save you a game once you start playing with the big boys.

There is another bust rule played around some boards. Say that in the same circumstances as before, you have thirty left, you hit a single 15 (leaving 15 to go), then the 17 by mistake, the score left on the scoreboard will be fifteen, not your original thirty. It sometimes works to your advantage, like if you're left with three to go, once you've hit the single 1 all that's left is the double 1, you cannot revert back to three again if you bust.

> Here are the perfect finishes for you to aim for while you practice or play.
> 101 — 2 darts Any player who can consistently finish with double these close-out
> 301 — 6 darts may consider himself a grand master.
> 501 — 9 darts
> 1001 — 17 darts
> (3 x 20 (15) 3 x 17 & 50)

Score Keeping

The tasks of the scorer are multifold. **Here is a list of the things he may do:**
* He may call out the score of each individual dart and the total score.
* He may tell the thrower how many points are required to finish the game.
* He may have the final decision on any controversy, such as who is nearest in the middle-for-diddle throw (starting bull shot).
* He may warn or disqualify the throw of a player stepping over the hockey.
* He may re-adjust the board if it is turned during the course of play.
* He may accept free drinks from both players or both teams.

The scorer must not do the following:
* Shout encouragement or blaspheme any player participating in a game.
* He may not tell the thrower what double he has left for a game, or advise on ways to finish.
* He must not stare at the man on the hockey.
* He must not hoot with laughter at a bad throw.
* He must not arbitrarily establish new rules against those agreed on prior to the start of the game.
* He must not accept free drinks in the form of a bribe from any one player.

The scorer should not really have any say in how the game is to be started, that is, which team starts. Local traditions or a huddle on the mat between the two teams usually decide the form of start. A common way is the 'middle-for-diddle'. If you don't know what that means then carefully read page 98.

The main problem with 'middle-for-diddle' is the hot players. They are both very likely to hit bulls and still leave the start up to contention, or land darts in the board which appear equidistant from the bull, in which case the decision is left in the hands of the scorer who or may not be one of your pals.

The two bulls problem can be settled by a loose tradition that defines the thrower who lands in the bull second as the winner of the ' middle-for-diddle ' as his target area was considerably smaller. 'Middle for diddle' does have its slight drawbacks but is nevertheless a splendid way of commencing a game whose outcome will not have too many international repercussions. But for top challenges another way has to be found. That grand affair, the News of the World Championships starts games with a toss of a coin. One school of thought is that tossing coins around has not the slightest connection with darts ability and the answer should not depend on pure luck. This holds a lot of truth.

A third way of trying to get a game started is that of each player shooting three arrows for the top total score. This can be a lengthy procedure when neither team can do better than 'bed and breakfast' (26). Should it be a team game and the team leader freaks out and hits a measly eleven after his opponent has just banged in one hundred eighty the effect on the team can be demoralizing.

Each of these three starting methods has its bad points. Oddly enough, the ideal unbiased start would be the flip a coin and the equal darts rules. It works like this: If the player who starts the leg should finish first, say in seventeen darts, his opponent, having only thrown fifteen darts would be entitled to attempt to win (in sixteen darts) or tie the game by closing out on his seventeenth dart.

With darts skill at such a high level nowadays when the difference between winning and losing an important game is often only one or two darts there should be more consideration given to this or a similar method of starting and finishing a leg.

Finally, before a 'Rubber' game the starting system should be repeated to determine who starts the final leg. We will now qualify a couple of statements we have made in this chapter to mollify the player who may have found something disagreeable.

Qualification 1

Starting the standard game doesn't always require a double. That's right. The "News of the World" finals, which are 501 games are straight starts. Maybe that is because they do not want to embarass the champions on the TV, they are under tremendous stress after all.

Qualification 2

Under one circumstance a player may throw twice at 'middle-for-diddle' i.e. if his first dart bounds out. Should his second attempt rebound he is not allowed a third try.

CHAPTER VI

Chase

(2 or 4 players, more could be a bore)

To illustrate this game and others, let's follow the throws of two veteran darts players — Harvey and Alf.

Also referred to as "American Cricket", "Mickey Mouse", "Sweaty Betty" and "Coach and Horses" and very likely a lot more names. Second in popularity only to the standard game, Chase has a lot to offer both the beginner and expert. In this game the ingredients of strategy, luck skill and quick thinking, are all boiled together to produce a winner. Good players are often beaten by the better strategist. And the lucky player can confound them both.

Each number shown represents scoring possibilities and the doubles and trebles are worth their usual value. The idea is to bring a number alive by hitting it three times. Any subsequent dart thrown into that number by the player with it alive scores. Three darts in the same number by the opponent, and it is dead — no longer in the game.

Right, middle-for-diddle.

Harvey starts and hits five 20's with his throw. This means he has brought 20's alive as only three of any number brings that number alive and earns three X's. Harvey got the three X's and with his other two 20's has scored forty points.

HARVEY   ALF

SCORE		B		SCORE
40	XXX	20		
		19		
		18		
		17		
		16		
		15		
		14		
		13		
		12		
		11		
		10		

Note that the game doesn't necessarily have to start on 20's; any number will do.

Three 20's bring the number alive, two more score 40.

Harvey is ahead on score 40 to 0, but now it is Alf's turn to throw. He comes to the hockey a bit of a worried man because he cannot register any score from 20's, his favorite bed. This leaves him with the following basic alternatives:

A)   He can chase Harvey by trying to kill his alive 20's to stop him from scoring again. To kill 20's he must get three X's on his side the board, a treble or a single + double, or three singles.

B)   He can decide that since he is forty points behind he should get another number alive from which he can pile in some score on his side. In this case 19's would be his best bet.

If Alf takes the defensive "A" course and succeeds in slipping three darts into the 20's this is what happens at the top of the board:

HARVEY			ALF
SCORE		B	SCORE
40	~~XXX~~	~~20~~	~~XXX~~
		19	
		18	
		17	
		16	
		15	
		14	
		13	
		12	
		11	
		10	

Now, Alf is of a bolder breed so he would naturally opt for alternative "B" to score and move onto the attack. This move is the most strategically sound for a good player as he could reverse the "Chase" aspect and not have to struggle through the next throws trying to kill Harvey's numbers.

Alf throws three very neat darts and groups in a treble 19 and two single 19's.

HARVEY				ALF
SCORE		B		SCORE
40	XXX	20		38
		19	XXX	
		18		
		17		
		16		
		15		
		14		
		13		
		12		
		11		
		10		

Three 19's for alive, two for score.
Now there is only two points difference.

76

● **What would Harvey do now?**

1)   He may want to stick with his two point lead and immediately proceed to kill Alf's 19's. By doing this he will have eliminated Alf's chance of scoring again in that bed and will have reduced Alf's options in his next throw to either killing 20's or opening a new number.

2)   Feeling that his two point lead is not sufficient Harvey could score more 20's; they are valuable, being the top scoring number. This could develop into a slinging match between 20's and 19's — unilluminating play and a sign of insecure players. But it could also work to force Alf onto the defensive making it obvious that 20's must be killed.

3)   Harvey is still in a slightly commanding position, so why not open up a new number. Getting the 18's alive would give him two score targets to Alf's one.

4)   If Harvey is feeling supremely confident he might try a quick shot at bulls, sealing off the end of the game and collecting any fallout from mis-shots going into other numbers.

5)   Harvey is an old sparring partner of Alf's and has a great respect for Alf's ability; he therefore may want to throw a combination of darts that will score and kill at the same time. One dart at 20's to lengthen his lead and the remaining two at 19's for a quick kill.

Harvey decides to take the option (1) route and proceeds to throw a single 19, a treble 19 and a treble 18.

HARVEY   ALF

SCORE		B		SCORE
40	XXX	20		38
	~~XXX~~	~~19~~	~~XXX~~	
	XXX	18		
		17		
		16		
		15		
		14		
		13		
		12		
		11		
		10		

Harvey is now in a strong position, being able to score on 18's or 20's, or open up numbers wherever he likes.

The above choice may seem apparent to the veteran Chase player but it is surprising how often the wrong selection of alternatives sways a game.

Many a sadly defeated team have had to reach into their pockets muttering "We should have killed those nineteens earlier on." A bit of thought beforehand is all that's needed.

Alf is now going to have his work cut out to level up on scoring potential, in the meantime doing a bit of killing. Not so easy with only three darts.

Thud, thud, thud.

It is a magnificent attempt, Alf has thrown a treble 17, a single 17 and treble 20. So the pendulum swings again with the golden 20's good 'n' dead and Alf with a 15 point advantage.

HARVEY   ALF

SCORE		B		SCORE
40	~~XXX~~	~~20~~	~~XXX~~	55
	~~XXX~~	~~19~~	~~XXX~~	
	XXX	18		
		17	XXX	
		16		
		15		
		14		
		13		
		12		
		11		
		10		

Alf: four 17's and a treble 20.

This game is going to be one of breathtaking excitement so we won't bore you with too much more commentary. You should have the general idea by now. So put your foot up on the bar rail and watch how the rest of the game goes.

HARVEY ALF

SCORE		B		SCORE
58	XXX	20	XXX	55
	XXX	19	XXX	
	XXX	18		
	XXX	17	XXX	
	X	16		
		15		
		14		
		13		

Harvey gets a single 18, a treble 17 and a single 16.

HARVEY ALF

SCORE		B		SCORE
58	XXX	20	XXX	
	XXX	19	XXX	71
	XXX	18	X	
	XXX	17	XXX	
	X	16	XXX	
		15		
		14		
		13		

Alf responds with four 16's and a single 18.

HARVEY ALF

SCORE		B		SCORE
	XXX	20	XXX	
76	XXX	19	XXX	71
	XXX	18	X	
	XXX	17	XXX	
	XXX	16	XXX	
		15		
		14		
		13		
		12		
		11		
		10		

Harvey senses the danger, scores and kills with a single 18 and two 16's

HARVEY   ALF

SCORE		B		SCORE
	XXX	20	XXX	
76	XXX	19	XXX	
	XXX	18	X	86
	XXX	17	XXX	
	XXX	16	XXX	
		15	XXX	
		14		
		13		
		12		
		11		
		10	XXX	

Alf ignores 18 and throws four 15's and treble 10's.

Note: The 'pies' 15/10 and 14/11 can be a turning point and a key factor in the outcome of the game. Being adjacent numbers they provide a jumbo size target.

Alf went for the extra fifteen to put himself back in the lead on score. Clever, because Harvey has now to deflect one or even two of his darts from the killing task in order to get back ahead on score.

HARVEY   ALF

SCORE		B		SCORE
	XXX	20	XXX	
	XXX	19	XXX	
94	XXX	18	X	86
	XXX	17	XXX	
	XXX	16	XXX	
	XXX	15	XXX	
		14		
		13		
		12		
		11		
	X	10	XXX	

Harvey — a treble 15, single 18 and single 10.

Alf underestimated Harvey, who, with some very versatile arrows scored and more or less wiped out the threat of the 15/10 pie, (by killing the 15's with a single dart in the treble) then scored on his 18's, and plonked his last dart into 10 for good measure.

HARVEY   **ALF**

SCORE		B		SCORE
	XXX	20	XXX	
	XXX	19	XXX	
94	XXX	18	XXX	96
	XXX	17	XXX	
	XXX	16	XXX	
	XXX	15	XXX	
		14		
		13		
		12		
		11		
	X	10	XXX	

Alf — two 18's and a 10.

A few grunts of disapproval from the bar for this throw. Alf very correctly killed the 18's with his first two darts but perhaps should have gone for the 14/11 pie with his third dart. Instead he earned a tenuous lead with a single 10. Harvey's next target is obviously going to be the 14/11 pie so Alf should have pre-empted him.

HARVEY   **ALF**

SCORE		B		SCORE
	XXX	20	XXX	
	XXX	19	XXX	
	XXX	18	XXX	
108	XXX	17	XXX	96
	XXX	16	XXX	
	XXX	15	XXX	
	XXX	14		
		13		
		12		
	X	11		
	X	10	XXX	

Harvey — four 14's and a single 11.

Alf pays for his mistake and Harvey ignores the 10's and concentrates on the 14/11 pie.

HARVEY   ALF

SCORE		B		SCORE
	XXX	20	XXX	
	XXX	19	XXX	
	XXX	18	XXX	
108	XXX	17	XXX	96
	XXX	16	XXX	
	XXX	15	XXX	
	XXX	14	XXX	
		13		
		12		
	X	11		
	X	10	XXX	

Alf — three 14's

Alf has put himself in the position where he has to chase and his throw leaves him still behind on score.

HARVEY   ALF

SCORE		B		SCORE
	XXX	20	XXX	
	XXX	19	XXX	
	XXX	18	XXX	
108	XXX	17	XXX	96
	XXX	16	XXX	
	XXX	15	XXX	
	XXX	14	XXX	
		13		
		12		
	XXX	11		
	XXX	10	XXX	

Harvey — three 10's, 11's.

Harvey, sensing victory, zooms in on the tens with a neat treble (overkill), then piles in the extra two elevens to give himself the important advantage of always having a number alive.

HARVEY   ALF

SCORE		B		SCORE
	XXX	~~20~~	XXX	
	XXX	~~19~~	XXX	
	XXX	~~18~~	XXX	
108	XXX	~~17~~	XXX	
	XXX	~~16~~	XXX	122
	XXX	~~15~~	XXX	
	XXX	~~14~~	XXX	
		13	XXX	
		12		
	XXX	11		
	XXX	~~10~~	XXX	

Alf — five 13's.

A beautiful response by Alf, a treble and two single 13's. Harvey must score at this stage to stop the gap from widening.

HARVEY   ALF

SCORE		B		SCORE
	XXX	~~20~~	XXX	
	XXX	~~19~~	XXX	
	XXX	~~18~~	XXX	
	XXX	~~17~~	XXX	
141	XXX	~~16~~	XXX	122
	XXX	~~15~~	XXX	
	XXX	~~14~~	XXX	
	XXX	~~13~~	XXX	
	X	12		
	XXX	11		
	XXX	~~10~~	XXX	

Harvey — treble 11,
treble 13 and a 12.

Harvey's hours of practice pay off with a great throw. Alf is now in trouble.

HARVEY   **ALF**

SCORE		B		SCORE
	XXX	20	XXX	
	XXX	19	XXX	
	XXX	18	XXX	
	XXX	17	XXX	
141	XXX	16	XXX	
	XXX	15	XXX	146
	XXX	14	XXX	
	XXX	13	XXX	
	X	12	XXX	
	XXX	11		
	XXX	10	XXX	

Alf — five 12's.

Alf is not about to admit defeat and with five 12's the balance of the game rocks wildly.

HARVEY   **ALF**

SCORE	X	B		SCORE
	XXX	20	XXX	
	XXX	19	XXX	
	XXX	18	XXX	
	XXX	17	XXX	
	XXX	16	XXX	146
152	XXX	15	XXX	
	XXX	14	XXX	
	XXX	13	XXX	
	XXX	12	XXX	
	XXX	11		
	XXX	10	XXX	

Harvey double 12, a single 11 and a cool Bull

Harvey goes convincingly back into the lead, on score and
strategic position.

HARVEY　　　　　　　　ALF

SCORE	X	B	XX	SCORE
	XXX	20	XXX	
	XXX	19	XXX	
	XXX	18	XXX	
	XXX	17	XXX	
	XXX	16	XXX	
152	XXX	15	XXX	146
	XXX	14	XXX	
	XXX	13	XXX	
	XXX	12	XXX	
	XXX	11		
	XXX	10	XXX	

Alf — Two single Bulls.

The game has now developed into a bullfight. Harvey can
safely ignore the 11's as he is ahead on score and two
more bulls will give him the game.　　Alf cannot win by
killing the 11's.

HARVEY　　　　　　　　ALF

SCORE	XXX	B	XX	SCORE
	XXX	20	XXX	
	XXX	19	XXX	
	XXX	18	XXX	
	XXX	17	XXX	
	XXX	16	XXX	
152	XXX	15	XXX	146
	XXX	14	XXX	
	XXX	13	XXX	
	XXX	12	XXX	
	XXX	11		
	XXX	10	XXX	

Harvey — double Bull.

That's it folks! As swift and clean as a surgeon Harvey slices his first dart into the bunghole. Finis.

Harvey wins by 152 to 146. As shown on the scoreboard, all numbers have been killed with the exception of 11's and bulls. There is no way Alf can get any more score, he can only kill.

To win

Harvey throughout the game, constantly kept the pressure on Alf by following the basic patterns that reflect winning strategy.
* He always captured the lead on score with his throw.
* He broke the 'pies' at the right time.
* He always left a number alive after his throw.
* He moved to kill numbers only when he had the score advantage.

To lose

These are the phsychological ingredients that go to making a loser. They don't apply in Alf's case who played an extremely good game:
* Lack of confidence in choosing and throwing for a number.
* Forgetting to analyze and respect the opponent's alternatives on the scoreboard.
* Maintaining a defensive attitude.
* Having no game plan and not working out the steps necessary to command a positive position at each stage of the game.

Handicaps

Chase can preserve its fun even when the players are not evenly matched. A handicap system is easy to apply. This can be done in two ways or, for that matter, a combination of both. The standard handicap is to simply mark up an agreed number on the weaker player's side of the scoreboard, usually, 100, 200 or 300.

The weaker player thus starts off the game ahead on score and has to concentrate more on killing to prevent his opponent from catching up.

The other type of handicap provides no beginning score but does allow a free mark (X) for each number prior to play.

If there is a staggering difference between the calibre of play between the two players the latter system plus a starting score can be used.

Team Play

Fun darts are even more fun when played by a group. It is more relaxing and casual and you don't have to shoulder all the blame if you lose. Chase is hard to beat as a team game as every element comes into it. Most teams are two a side but up to eight a side is not unknown.

The basic rules and objectives are the same for team play as for individual play, but there are a few twists in strategy to think about.

First of all you need a team captain. This honor is usually reserved for a better darts player as he has some heavy responsibilities, which happily don't include having to buy all the drinks for the winners.

* Negotiating the game's rules.
* Deciding his team's order of play, if only two on the team then the other fellow throws second.
* Hitting the bunghole in a middle-for-diddle start.
* Planning and directing the strategy for each member of his team.
* Settling with the opposing captain any disputes arising from play.

In team play the captain must keep his eye on the score-board (and on his drink in some pubs) and make decisions fast. He also has to analyze the opposition's capabilities in relation to those of his own team, often discouraging but necessary as the rotation factor is highly important. For example, the weakest member should be directed to throw defensively if he is followed by the opposition's best player. This is a common sense move as you can't expect a duffer to establish leads for the team.

Chase Nomination

A more demanding variation for the better players among us. Chase Nomination is exactly the same as the regular game of Chase with one exception: prior to each throw, or dart, the player on the hockey has to nominate, loud and clear, the number that he is intending to hit. Complete frustration is the reward for lack of accuracy, since numbers hit other than those nominated are scored on the opponent's side.

For example, Harvey calls his beloved 20's before he throws and correctly gets two single 20's but misses widely with his third dart which swings off and lands in the 12's. As he nominated 20's as his target the 12 mis-shot goes on the opponent's side of the scoreboard.

The game gets tricky when it comes to going for the 15/10, 14/11 combinations. A slight miss will score for the opponent. A safe approach is to aim toward the doubles in this case.

Another dicy area is the bull. If other numbers are still alive and a player nominates the bull, an arrow on the wrong side of the wire could score for his opponent or help kill one of his own alive numbers.

NOTE: *A player may change his call before any dart. He can nominate 20's for his first arrow, throw, then call 19's for his second, throw, then switch to another number for his last dart.*

Chase Hong Kong Style

Another fascinating version, the same in concept and procedure as the regular game of Chase with two exceptions.

* Until 20's are alive no other number can be aimed for. To begin the game, therefore, every dart must be on the 20 trajectory. Thus, the start of the game is critical as 20's are everybody's focal point. The side hitting three 20's may proceed to score, or move on to another number. The other side must kill the 20's before they can start moving through the scoreboard. Only 20's have this limitation.

* There are no 11's and 10's in the Hong Kong game, so it follows that there are no easy 'pies'.

This foreshortened version of Chase originated in Hong Kong owing to the big waiting lists on every board on the island (darts are the second most popular form of entertainment in the crowded colony).

Chase Supreme

Also referred to as "Super Mouse' and 'The DT's'. Again, the basic concept is the same as the regular game but there is a significant difference. The 10's and 11's are replaced by doubles (D) and trebles (T), making the scoreboard look like this:

		B		
		20		
		19		
		18		
		17		
		16		
		15		
		14		
		13		
		12		
		T		
		D		

The substitution of doubles and trebles raises the strategic elements of the game as well as calling for more marksmanship.

In Super Mouse, all the doubles and trebles on the board are active. For instance, if it is Alf's hot night on trebles and he throws two treble 20's and a treble 1, after he has wept for joy he has to start thinking about the options open to him.

He can,

a)   count all three darts as trebles and make the 'T's' alive (XXX) or,

b)   take one of his treble 20's and put three X's in the 20 column and two XX's in the 'T' column, or,

c)   he can stick with the one treble 1 (for one X against 'T') and count the six 20's as XXX plus a sixty score.

His choice would depend almost entirely on how he evaluates the capabilities of his opposition.

Advantageous use of the trebles and doubles often decides the winner in a tight game of Super Mouse.

Doubles and trebles are the most rewarding areas and a player who can get the DT's alive can expect a free beer in his near future. Once alive, any double or treble on the board counts for score, worth a lot of points.

The wrong decision at the right time can lose the game. A lot of fingernails can be chewed away trying to decide whether to take a double or treble as a score, a kill, or a X, but it makes Super Mouse great entertainment.

NOTE: *The same applies with the DT's as with other numbers, they may be killed by the opposition with three reciprocating X's.*

Remember also that the bunghole has double value, but the outer bull only counts as a single and the usual twenty-five points.

CHAPTER VII

Traditions & Terminology

The unwritten laws of darts.

Traditions, ettiquette, courtesies, customs . . . and a rule. The traditions of darts have grown out of the necessity for some kind of regulation without the rigidity of set rules, and also because people throughout the ages have found that a few traditions allow for more gamesmanship in the sport.

One of the more notable aspects of this sport is the notable absence of standard rules.

There are plenty of flexible traditions, but when it comes to rules we find them happily absent. Even the world's major competition, the News of the World Championships, lists only ten rules, three of which refer to the conduct of the spectators and six of which describe the aspects of scoring or refereeing for that particular competition. Only one, relative to standing behind the hockey, can really be classified as a playing rule. In normal pub play, basic rules for the game are agreed upon beforehand, and in the event of a controversy, the decision is left in the hands of the referee, scorer or pub owner or bartender.

Sometimes, rules have to be established to cover unusual circumstances. 'Humpin' is one of these. When a dart sticks into the rear end of one dart already in the board it is called 'humpin', and though this is the ultimate in good grouping, the second dart has no scoring value.

Another is in the event of the dart tucking itself under the wire of an old board with loose spiders. If your dart plops into a twenty but the point has buried itself under the ring and into treble twenty, sorry, but you only get a single twenty. The rule states that the score is taken from the place where the dart first hits the face of the board.

*"These locals seem to have
their own set of rules"*

If you accidentally drop a dart from the hockey you may retrieve it and throw it. Only darts reaching a plane level with the face of the board are valid. Any player dropping a dart three times during the course of one throw should lose one dart from his throw. (He should also have some strong black coffee poured down his throat.)

As a general rule the score of all darts are counted if they are still in the board when the player moves away from the hockey. Alternatively if the scorer has called "game shot" and the dart then falls out, the game is counted as over. If you can see your first or second dart is hanging precariously in the board and anticipate it falling out, you can disregard its score and continue throwing at the previous target. Should the dart then fall out with the subsequent pounding, you are left in a desirable position, especially if you are after a game shot. Of course if the dart does not fall out you may have problems.

So, apart from the oddball circumstances, here is a sport in essence without rules, but this doesn't mean mayhem reigns around every board.

Traditions hold the game together, and unlike rules, they are not obligatory, such as the tradition that says the losers buy the winners a drink, a mere pleasantry that saves fist fights and ill will.

These traditions generally cover playing conduct and unfortunately seem to be becoming noticeably absent in quite a few games nowadays. It should be the intention of every dart player to acquaint newcomers with the unwritten laws of darts so that the sport may continue to grow in an atmosphere of goodwill and fellowship.

● **Tradition one:**

Remove your own darts, and let other players remove theirs.

Perhaps one of the first unwritten laws of the game is that every player should always, always, remove his own darts from the board, unless: a) he has suffered a heart attack after scoring 180 (in which case his score still counts for the team), or b) he is too short to reach up to the board in which case he may appoint a caddie, but only if there's not a bar stool handy to climb on.

Many darts players strongly dislike somebody taking out their darts, especially if it is a novice who may crumple his carefully manicured flights, and in particular somebody who has just removed his hand from a bag of greasy french fries.

● **Tradition two:**

Never play with another person's darts without permission of the owner. To most good players their darts are sacred and most devotees would rather lend you their wife than their arrows. Most taverns should keep a good stock of durable plastic flighted darts for the use of the casual chucker.

● **Tradition three:**

Introductions all around before a game. Starting off in an easy friendly atmosphere leads to a more enjoyable game every time and it is far better to mark the board Peter and Paul versus Tom and Jerry then merely writing 'A' & 'B' or 'Them' and 'Us', as sometimes happens.

● **Tradition four:**

Sing out your score. After all your darts have hit you should, in most cases, be able to tell from the hockey what you have scored. Singing out the score gives your opponents a chance to verify it and saves any doubt. Scurrying to the board, whipping out your darts and scribbling a number down may lead to suspicion.

You may be as honest as George Washington but nobody likes to be accused of cheating on the score. If a dart has landed close to a wire and its position is unclear, tap it with your hand away from the wire and call out its score before removing it. Also, if your darts are all closely clustered in the bull allow your opponents to have a good look. It's their privilege, particularly if they are going to buy you a drink for the game shot.

- **Tradition five:**

Do not lean across to see where somebody's dart has landed. This is not only discourteous but it is also a good way to get a dart in the back of your head. Any kind of distraction is extremely bad form. Wait until the throw has been completed before checking the score. Also shouting out a score, unless requested by the thrower, is bad form.

- **Tradition six:**

Do not talk to any man about to throw. It may be funny to ask him the time just as he is aiming for a game shot but it does not contribute to the spirit of the game. Lots of chatter surrounding the board in a bar is quite normal but direct comments about the thrower's shoes, necktie, etc., and other forms of heckling drag the sport down to a·very low level.
Banned from the game are all forms of harrassment aimed at the man on the hockey. Such common tricks as 'accidentally' dropping your darts (especially into the thrower's foot), whistling, glaring into the thrower's face and rattling ice cubes all count as behaviour deserving of a disqualification, or at least some form of penalty. The kinds of penalties you can give for deliberate foul play we will leave to your own imagination.

- **Tradition seven:**

Next man to play should keep score. It is more or less the duty of anybody awaiting his turn at the board to keep score for the people playing before them.
The game moves along at a faster clip this way and the unprejudiced marker can also act as a referee. Also the players don't get chalky hands.

- **Tradition eight:**

In general pub play the winning team or individual stays on the board. This is the accepted norm in most non-tournament games and the 'next up' is the man who has been keeping score, or his team.

● **Tradition nine:**
Win and lose with equal pride. Do not make alibis or blame the scorer when you are beaten and don't brag or boast when you win. This is probably a standard tradition for all sports, but for darts it seems to have a more special application. As the game has always been connected with pleasure and relaxation, a hostile crowd around the board can destroy a pub's atmosphere.

> "For when the one Great Scorer comes to write against your name he marks not that you won or lost but how you played the game."

Terminology:

Although a lot of terminology heard around some boards would make a longshoreman blush, there are a collection of ripe old expressions and words, all perfectly respectable, handed down from generation to generation of darts players that are the heritage of the sport.
In order to preserve these fine old sayings, since they certainly add a touch of flavor and character to the sport, we suggest everybody tuck a few away in his mental labyrinth ready to pop out when the time is right. Apart from giving you the opportunity at a bit of one-upmanship, a good working knowledge of these colorful sayings can prepare you for the time when you meet that funny little Cockney player. At the very least it will enable you to communicate with him in a limited way and you won't be left bewildered as he struts around crying such seeming obscenities as "Hard Cheddar, gov'ner, now split the legs!"
Just as the disciples of baseball, football, basketball, golf, etc. can leave the layman dumbfounded by a stream of their jargon, with this stock of choice phrases the dartplayer can hold his own, confusing the bystander while displaying his intimate knowledge of the game. The

authors take no responsibility for any incidents should cries such as "Three in a bed, up in Annie's room" be misconstrued.

Arrow — A dart, ref. Chapter II

Away — To "Get Away" doesn't mean "buzz off" in the darts player's language but to get started. "Away" = started, so "He's away" simply means "He's started" and is also usually used as "40 away" or "36 away". i.e. started on double top or double 18.

Annie's room, up in — The number 1 on the board.

Bill Harvey — Don't ask why, but it means 100.

Birds — (U.K.) Non-feathered bystanders now and again seen in skirts. Will sometimes want to join in a game. Amusing to have around, and especially useful as scorekeepers if kept supplied with free drinks. In this age of liberation many are threatening to take up this warrior's sport professionally.

The Bull — Anywhere in the two center circles.

Black Bull — A double bull

The Bunghole — A double bull

The Button — See "The Bunghole"

Bed, Three in — Three darts in any one of the treble or double segments, or in the inner 'bull.

Bed & Breakfast — A bed for the night and breakfast used to cost 2 shillings and 6 pence (2 and 6 ~ 26) in British traverns. Single 20, single 1, and single 5, amounting to a score of twenty-six in three darts. A score often achieved amongst the ranks of beginners and average players while trying to hit 20's.

To Best — To overscore, time to "Come out".

Caned — If you've been caned you've undergone a humiliating defeat. Don't be humiliated, whitewash him next game. "Caned", meaning whipped with a cane, is not to be confused with "Canned", you could be arrested for the latter but not for the former.

A Chucker — One with the inability to grasp the finer points of throwing styles.

Clock — The dartboard with numbers from 1 ~ 20.

Come Out — Your opponent overscores while attempting to finish so you merrily shout "Come out", and receive a black look in reply. Merely means "Hard Cheddar, you've bust". "Too Hot", equal in meaning. Do not confuse with "Get out".

Double Top — Double 20's.

Downstairs-Bottom of the board. This is where the biggest group of odd numbers lies, 7, 19, 3, 17.

Dosser — See the "Button".

Dry Wipe—Winning the first two legs out of three consecutively, thus winning the game.

Game Shot — The final and winning dart of a game.

Get Out — To finish the game. "He got out on double top" = he finished the game on double 20's, sometimes used as a noun, 'a get-out'.

Hard Cheddar — Tough luck.

Hockey — Throwing line.

Hops — Your round called when a game is lost and a reminder to the loser that he buys the drinks. Running around shouting "Hops, Hops!" nowadays may only get you a big thirst, or a job as a bunny.

Humpin' — With uncapped darts it often happens that one dart will stick in the end of another dart already in the board, this is "Humpin" and doesn't qualify for any score. The same applies for darts which wedge between the shaft and the adaptor of a landed dart.

Kelly's Eye — Number 1 on the clock.

A Leg — A completed score of 301 or 501. Three legs make one full game.

Leg and Leg — When each side has won a leg each. Same as Level Pegging.

Level Pegging — Each with equal scores or with scores very close to each other after every round of throws. A very close contest from start to finish.

Madhouse — Double one.

Middle-for-Diddle — A beautiful old expression and probably the favorite of darts players everywhere. Throwing for the bull to establish who starts the game. Usually termed as a polite question to one's opponent after a few warm-up throws. "Middle for Diddle?" — "Shall we start?"

Mugs Away — Equally popular. Losers of the previous game to start off the next one. Also couched as an invitation to play another leg, given from the winning team, or player. Doesn't really mean "Do you mugs want to play again?" So shouldn't be said with a smirk. It has a more gentlemanly meaning — "As you appear to have lost the last game would you care to accept the privilege of starting a new one?"

Numbers	0	—	Oxo
	9	—	Doctor's Favorite
	10	—	Downing Street
	11	—	Legs
	21	—	Key of the Door
	22	—	Swans on the Lake
	22	—	Dinkey Doo
	22	—	Fried Fish
	22	—	Two Little Ducks
	26	—	Half a Crown
	26	—	Bed and Breakfast
	33	—	Feathers
	45	—	Bag o'nuts
	57	—	Heinz (or Varieties)
	66	—	Clickety Click
	76	—	Trombones
	77	—	Sunset Strip
	88	—	Connaught Rangers
	88	—	Golden Gates
	100	—	A Ton
	111	—	Lord Nelson

Off the Island—Off the board, or at least outside the double ring.

Old Ladies (or Pies)—Combinations of 11 & 14 and also 10 & 15. This term is used in the game of Chase, as both numbers lie together on the board. A mis-shot at one will likely hit the next-door number and score accidentally. In the game strategy, "Old Ladies" make a natural big target for the weaker player.

On your Knees—Go after double 3. Could also mean, 'since you've got us down to such a lousy double you better pray you hit it'.

The Pug—See "The Dosser".

A Point—See "Arrow".

To Rip—Used in the standard game indicating the number remaining has to be broken down so you can finish on a double. For example, '35 to rip' means you have to hit an odd number, say 3, and then the double (16), or any other combination. In brief, two darts away from finishing the game.

The Rubber—The third and/or final leg of a game that will decide the winner.

Shanghai—After the darts game of Shanghai. Often used in friendly games to get out other than by the usual finish. Constitutes a single, double, and treble, in that order of any one number. The thrower has to shout "Shanghai" before going for the treble, and have the proposition accepted by the opposition. If he misses he loses any score made in that throw, and he may also lose a drink if that is the wager.

Spiders—The wires

Split the Legs—In a friendly game one is often left with a score of two (double one) to finish on and in attempting to hit the double he puts the dart into the single one. Normally, since he is left with one point, he would be considered as having bust since he can't throw for a double ½ on his next turn. He can, however, call for "Splitting the legs". If his opponent approves, he can throw one arrow for the number eleven which is horizontal on the left side of the board. If he can put this arrow between the two one digits of the number 11, then he can win the game.

The Throw—'A throw' is three darts at the board. As against 'A dart' — one dart at the board.

Ton—A score of one hundred. Other scores: a ton-twenty (120), a ton-thirty (130), etc. Presumably taken from the fact that there are twenty hundredweights in one ton weight.

Top of the House— Double twenty. Also 'Top of the Shop'.

Wet Feet—Foot fault. Toes in front of, or in some critical circles touching, the hockey. In championship games the toes must not even touch the hockey. In friendly games 'wet feet' is not cause for a disqualified throw unless done too blatantly.

Whitewash—As used in other sports, means to get beaten by your opponent without your having registered a score, or (better) vice versa. Doubles the drinks won.

Wrong Bed—Stumbling into the wrong apartment after a heavy night with the boys, or, as related to darts, hitting the next door number instead of the intended target. Mostly used when the wrong double or treble is hit.

You've been—You've overscored. Careful with this one, some bruiser may not like to be reminded.

You're Off—Your turn to start.

It is hoped that these expressions, however quaint some may sound, can get firmly planted in the American game and anyone with the patience and interest to learn them will initiate his friends.

Customs:

Catcher's

Many a dart viciously rebounds from the wire, scattering bystanders, or now and again impaling a foot. Throwers with long reaches and fast reflexes may take advantage of these darts under customs existing in some localities. Any dart on the rebound may be caught by the thrower and rethrown, this is providing he does not step over the hockey to catch the dart. Incidentally, it is a good idea to keep some cotton wool and a bottle of antiseptic behind the bar. Darts not caught, naturally, are nonscoring darts but for those retrieved the subsequent score from the re-throw is valid.

Darts Ladder

Most every pub has a house darts ladder. It is a per-manently active challenge list for regular players to establish their abilities against each other. The ladder is usually confined to ten or twelve players and posted on a wall near the dart area for easy viewing. It is usually made of wood with sliding panels that can be interchanged reflecting any change in ranking. The man on top is con-sidered the house champion. Although the requirements differ from pub to pub, there is usually some time element that requires each person on the ladder to defend his position every two weeks or so.

At the same time, a player on the list cannot refuse a challenge — to do so forfeits his position automatically. A challenge may come from two positions on the ladder. The standard challenge is the one that comes from the player directly under the one above. If the challenger wins, they exchange positions on the ladder. The other challenge can come from the second down on the ladder. For instance, if the ladder reads as follows:

Harvey
Alf
Bud

Jerry
Fred

And Bud challenges Harvey and wins, then the position on the ladder will be adjusted as follows:

Bud
Alf
Harvey
Jerry
Fred

However, should Bud lose in his challenge, he would have to drop a position on the ladder:

Harvey
Alf
Jerry
Bud
Fred

Besides providing a perpetual competition that regulates itself, the darts ladder is also a good yardstick in selecting competent members to represent the pub's darts team.

The Gallon

In team play, it is the custom to play one game of 1001 with all members participating and the losing team obliged to pick up the tab for a gallon of beer. The 1001 is a straight start with a double finish and all players must rotate according to the team line-up. It is believed that since a team usually consists of eight playing members, the origin of this expression is perhaps associated with eight players buying eight pints, equivalent to a gallon.

Honor Roll

Most pubs are proud of the historical events witnessed under their rafters. Granted, such happenings in a pub may not change the course of the world, but they could be recognized as being a step in that direction. Many pubs have a posted plaque or notice referred to as the Darts Honor Roll showing the listing of various players (with dates) who have been successful in scoring the coveted 180. Another Darts Honor Roll may have a listing of those players who have scored three double bulls, which is a distinction that could compare with, say, a hole-in-one in golf.

> Landlords, get that board up. Rough estimates disclose that as much as $3 million per *week* pour into British publican's pockets as a result of the game of darts.

Landlord's Pint

A grand old tradition not always adhered to by modern pub owners. Any player scoring 180 in three darts during the course of a game (note: not while practicing) qualifies for a free drink on the house. To encourage the game in their establishments publicans should not let traditions such as this fall by the wayside. Unless the bar is the home ground of champion players he won't have to give out many free pints during the course of a year. The Condor's Bar in Hongkong used to give a free bottle of Scotch for the 180 feat. Unfortunately they no longer keep up with this generous tradition, partly due to one of the authors of this book who took home five or six bottles in a single month.

Penny in the Box

During the course of play in any game of 301, 501, 1001, etc. a player who scores eleven or less total score with his three darts is likely to hear the call — "Penny in the box". (The eleven or under score does not apply when one is going after a double to start or end the game.) Any player with a sense of honor (humor) should oblige by dropping a penny in the box specially built for the occasion. The revenue gained on the contributed pennies is usually donated to the pub's darts team which, in turn, is used to off-set some of the expenses incurred from their weekly matches such as travel, food, drink, prizes, fines, etc.

Scorer's Pleasure

Most people regard the act of scorekeeping as an unrewarding job. There is a time, however, when the scorer is ceremoniously recognized for his labors. This is done quite by accident. When the two players or teams are playing 301 and both scores *recorded on the board*, after a round, are identical between 200 and 100, the player having just thrown should be obliged to provide a pint for the scorer.

Symbolism

A brush, drawn on the board under the player's name indicates a whitewash (also a Tin Hat or Egg). Some players like to try and rattle their opponents when a whitewash is in sight by filling in the brush in stages, drawing in the handle then gradually filling in the bristles as the whitewash becomes more and more imminent. Harmless but not really cricket.

Quickies

Many pubs have different traditions that liven up the game. One of these is the quick game endings. Most well known in this category is *Shanghai* which consists of throwing a single, treble and double in any one segment. (Refer page 128). Another game quickie is the *Three in a Bed*. Any time a player is able to throw his three darts in the *same* doubles bed or in the *same* trebles bed, then a short-cut to victory is attained.

The only exception to this tradition is in the game of 301 whereby this achievement is only accepted provided the score does not bust. (If a player has 163 to go out and throws three treble twenties, he will have bust and neither the score nor his three-in-a-bed has a recognized value).

Still yet another quickie is the treble terror numbers of one and two in the game of 301. (Also three and four if playing 501). If a player, upon approaching the hockey, verbally notes that his score *shown on the board* is 111 or 222, he can request permission from his opponent to have a go at the treble terror.

If his opponent consents, a one dart throw is allowed for the number in question. (If 111 is left, the one dart must be placed in the treble one — if 222 is left, one dart must be placed in the treble two.) If that particular treble is hit, then the game is abruptly ended. If missed, the value scored by that one dart is deducted from the thrower's score and his remaining two darts are forfeited on that round.

Even the Japanese have their own interpretation of a quickie. There is a pub in Tokyo, Eri's Cabin by name, that has a five yen piece placed just outside the playing area of the board.

The five yen piece has a center hole which is about one-quarter the size of the double bull. A dart placed in this center at any stage of the game will result in an automatic win. This approach has its drawbacks as it very quickly destroys the points of the darts.

The reader must be reminded that all of the above close-outs are traditions, to be used only in friendly dart play. They are *not* standard practices for competition games.

CHAPTER VIII

---

23 Popular Games

One of the most interesting aspects of darts is the enormous variety of games that can be played without a single change in equipment or facilities. A slight amount of imagination and bonhomie can transform a dull evening with a bunch of mediocre players into a night of unlimited excitement.

There are probably as many different games and variations as there are pubs in the British isles — and then some. It would take an encyclopedia to list and fully describe them all. We have therefore included in the next few pages a few of the most popular games that are played and enjoyed in various parts of the world, and that earn the most number of hangovers. We think they are a fair selection and their popularity where they are played qualifies them as accepted 'standard' games. The word 'standard' is used reluctantly as the true darts player considers only one game as being the standard game. Let there be no misunderstanding — 301, 501, 801, 1001 are *the* games of darts — no ifs or buts.

To allow you to relax from the pressures of playing world championship stuff and play for the pure clean fun of hurling arrows at a board should be justification enough for listing all these games. The varying degree of skill and versatility required is a better reason for your giving them a try; the real darts player should be an all round man ready to take up his weapons no matter who blows the clarion.

All games have been classified according to their difficulty and we would hereby like to establish a new international standards designation — DDD (degree of darts difficulty). DDD is determined on the basis of the precision required by a player to hit his intended target with at least one of his three darts.

DDD gradings are on the star system and can be interpreted as follows:

One star (*)

Game for the raw beginner. Players who have just introduced themselves to the sport and have only a few games and no wins to their credit. (There are some, you know).

Throughout play these games do not require the throwing of a double, treble or bull.

Two stars (**)

For the beginner with a record of three or four weeks regular playing, 6 to 8 drinks won, and showing definite signs of improvement. Introduction of trebles and doubles in these games adds more of a challenge.

Three stars (***)

Fun for the average player, and a mixture of skill and luck for everyone, especially in team play where talent can be off-set. Basically intended for the player who has at least 500 flight hours in his log, has worn out five sets of flights, and is beginning to get his wife interested in darts.

Fours stars (****)

These games have appeal for the better than average darts player and for the average player who thinks he's better than average. Skill is heavily demanded to be a convincing and consistent winner. Best for players who can hold their own on a local team; have at least a couple of years experience; won enough beer to float a good-size ketch, and have raised stirrings of interest in the game with their mothers-in-law. Doubles, trebles and bulls decide the outcome of these games and a good player should have the ability to hit one of these with one out of every three darts.

Five stars (*****)

Masters stuff. Competitive scoring in these games is accomplished only by precision. For professionals, non-professional champions, MD's and BA's*.

* MD = Master Dartsman, BA = Brilliant Arrowist.

107

Players in this category probably had a board at the end of their crib; in their careers have won enough beer to float a battleship (and it shows); and have been left by their wives and now practice regularly with their mothers-in-law.

We will again use Harvey and his friend Alf to illustrate how these games should be played. Harvey is an MD at the sport and Alf is a well-qualified BA (sometimes called an MF by his closer friends). They both therefore throw a mean arrow so don't be surprised at the hot pace they set.

We can promise you that many a dart night will be enlivened by the introduction of one or two of these games. If you don't enjoy any of them you can stick the back page of this book on the board and throw at the authors.

Killer (DDD ***)

Also known as "Gang-Bang" as any number can play, in fact the more the merrier. A jolly, vindictive game with each player looking after his own interests. Often heartbreaking for a good player as he finds himself the natural target for every other players' arrows.

● **To Start.**

Each player selects his number by throwing with the opposite hand, usually left. If he's an ambidextrous natural athlete he can use his left foot. The number hit is his assigned number throughout the game. If either the first, second, third or fourth dart don't go in the board he may retire back to his bar stool. Each participant throws until every player on the scoreboard has a *different* number.

Bulls are also counted as a number, though not advisable, first because they are awfully tough to hit throwing with your left foot, and also because . . . but we shall come to that later. The player with the lowest number receives the privilege of starting the game, with the other players following in numerical sequence.

Let's put Jerry, Harvey, Alf and Percy on the mat to show you around the game of Killer.

Players	No.	Lives
Jerry	2	1 1 1
Harvey	5	1 1 1
Alf	11	1 1 1
Percival	17	1 1 1

All players have designated their numbers, each has three lives. Once a player has lost all his lives he is automatically out of the game and his only value is his beer-purchasing power for the winner.

● **To Score.**
Jerry starts as his number is the lowest (2). His first objective is to establish himself as a Killer. He becomes a Killer only by hitting the double 2, his number. He may go for this with his natural throwing arm. If he successfully hits the double 2 he earns a big fat K on the scoreboard indicating he has become a Killer, and a man to be feared.

He can then proceed to try to kill the other players by hitting their doubles. So the lives of Percy, Harvey and Alf are in danger.

A bit of care is also necessary for a Killer because if he should accidentally swing a dart into his own double again he would be committing harakiri by taking one of his own lives. In Jerry's case he'd better steer clear of Percy's 17's as his own 2 is only a wire away.

The next man to hit his own double also becomes a Killer so now the two players not yet alive have their problems which will only be solved when they can get onto the attack. The game gets really exciting when all players have become Killers. This is the time when flattery, threats and drinks change hands freely as players gang-up to persecute a player or win a stay of execution. But no matter what allies are formed in mid-game the end is inevitably a dog-eat-dog affair.

Two rules to note:

1. If a player is able to throw a double with his first, opposite-hand throw he is assigned that number and immediately starts off as a Killer.

2. If a player is able to hit a bull with his opposite hand

throw then he needs a double bull to become a Killer. In turn, the other players can only rob him of his lives by hitting double bull.

In this game bull is often a bad idea. No other player can put his own number in jeopardy, or those of his friends, by going for the bull. So the bull man is an outcast and is likely to have all the players ranged against him.

● **To win**
* Keep quiet.
* Don't antagonize anybody.
* Miss your own doubles for as long as is safely possible, i.e. until you see somebody else is aiming for them.
* In a group of strangers pretend you are not the doubles genius you really are, don't try and eliminate everybody else single-handed. Let them kill off each other.
* Keep the best player liberally supplied with free drinks.
* Promote inter-rivalry between the other players. For example you may quietly imply to them that you've heard rumours that the best player has been seen around town with their girlfriends and/or wives.

Football: Version I (DDD *****)

Can be played by two people but benefits from the pressure of team competition. Each team is represented by one of the twenty segments on the board. In this respect, twenty players could feasibly be represented should match play be of interest.

Prior to the middle–for–diddle, both players or teams must agree on the number of goals required to win the game, or set a time limit.

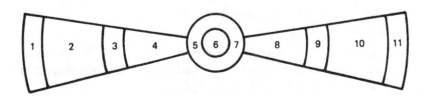

A goal is scored by the player starting on his own double and continuing through his opponent's segment to his double. It therefore takes a minimum of eleven darts to obtain one goal. First to score wins the game. Players alternate their throws and carry on where they left off. Note the sequence required: Own double, large single, treble, small single, outer bull, inner bull, outer bull, opponent's small single, treble, large single and *double — score*. For weaker players this game is a long hard plod across the board with little scoring action.

Soccadarts (DDD ****)

A brand new game with lots of interest and potential. This is a transatlantic game, merging the principles of American football with the rules of English soccer.

Until now it has mainly been played regularly by the authors and now and again, with an accommodating Japanese landlord called Taka. All innocent bystanders who have been pressed into a game have loved it. We are sure you will.

It makes an ideal practice game for you and a friend, but is not really for a beginner as the precision demanded limits scoring.

The rules may appear a bit complex at first, but a couple of games and you should have them off by heart.

● **To start.**

Get hold of a good darts companion and mark the scoreboard like this:

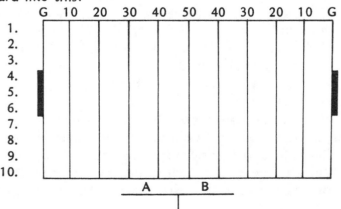

All those vertical lines will be familiar to the exfootball players; each one represents 10 yards. Total distance is therefore 100 yards.

The numbers 1 through 10 on the left of the scoreboard are the throws for each player. Ten throws each make up half a game. You could shorten the game by having five throws per half, but you have to be good to score in five throws. Finally, leave a place somewhere on the board to record goals.

We kick off with a 'middle-for-diddle'. The winner has possession of the ball which is, as usual, on the center 50 yard line.

Let's see Harvey and Alf again in action with Harvey in possession. With his three darts he has to get as big a score as possible (double and trebles count their respective values).

Harvey gets a 52 total.

Now it is Alf's throw.

Alf scores a 60.

So with the first play Alf scores eight points more than Harvey and has taken the ball away from him and moved it 8 yards towards Harvey's goal. The higher score takes possession of the ball.

*   The objective of each player is to move the ball down the field to where they can take a kick at goal.

*   If a player can move the ball towards the opponent's goal and land on or between the 21 yard line and the 30 yard line he qualifies for a goal attempt.

*   To score a goal from the above position requires the hitting of a double bull with one dart. (Goal score is worth one point.)

*   If a player can move the ball closer to the opponent's goal — between the goal line and the 20 yard line — he also qualifies for a goal attempt. To score he must throw one dart anywhere in the bull, double or single. (Again, the goal score is worth one point).

● **Back to the game.**

Alf is on the 42 yard line and has possession of the ball.

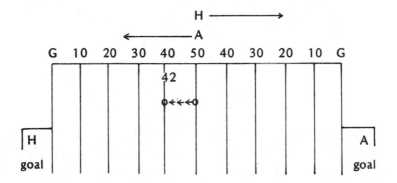

Let us mention at this point that score marking requires a bit of neatness to avoid confusion later. The best way is to mark individual scores and results at the left side like this:

1. H − 52
    A − 60   A + 8

Record the position of the ball on the field as shown, with a circled number giving yardage from the opponent's goal.

The game has started again, and we are on No. 2 play with Alf in possession as he won the first play, therefore he throws first this time.
Alf scores a total of 55.
Harvey scores a big 83.

So Harvey is 28 points up on Alf this time and he gets possession and streaks 28 yards down the field.

The left hand side of the board will now read:

1. H − 52
    A − 60   A + 8

2. A − 55
    H − 83   H + 28

The scoreboard records this move.

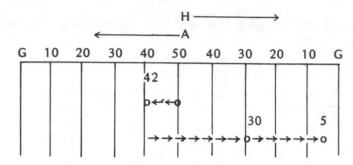

In landing on the 30 yard line, Harvey has qualified himself for a goal attempt. (a double bull with one dart is required on or between the 21 and 30 yard line)

Harvey, unfortunately, misses his goal shot and lands in the single bull. Thus, the ball is moved an equivalent 25 yards down the field to the 5 yard line.

Scores from goal shots are not recorded in the left column, only on the field. As Harvey missed his goal shot he has lost possession of the ball and it remains where it landed, on the 5 yard line.

With Alf in possession the next play starts as before.

3.   A − 45   H + 1
       H − 46

Harvey has again taken the initiative from Alf by outscoring him and stealing the ball. He moves one yard forward and qualifies for another attempt at goal. This time any bull, inner or outer, scores.

Note: *Alf's mediocre score of 45 meant that Harvey had to be a little bit careful. He controlled his score by hitting two 20's and then a 6. Since the ball was on the 5 yard line Harvey did not want to overscore and push it over the goal line with a score greater than 50, which would have lost him his chance for a goal attempt.*

Harvey has his next try at a bull.

Zap. Missed by a whisker and into single 17.

This 17 puts him over the goal line and the scoreboard now appears as follows, with the ball somewhere in the stands.

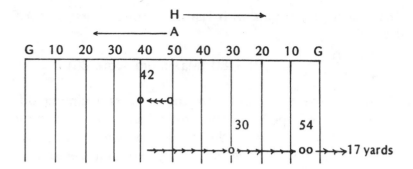

It is now Alf's ball and his goal kick from the goal line. He has three darts to gain a score that will get the ball clear from the goal line.

He proceeds to throw two 20's and a 5 — total 45. On a goal kick the ball is moved a yardage equivalent to the total score thrown . . . the opponent has no control over the distance but takes possession of the ball after the throw.

So Harvey has the ball on Alf's 45 yard line.

Note: *A 45-yard goal kick is a poor show on Alf's behalf as with a good score he could have moved the ball all the way down to the other goal line. The goal kick is a chance for the team under pressure to reverse the tables. At the same time, throwing a goal kick must be somewhat controlled as a whopping score over 100 will send the ball flying over the opposite goal line and a call for a return goal kick.*

The board at this point reads:

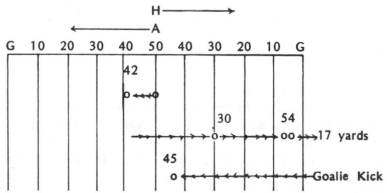

The fourth play begins with Harvey throwing first and Alf defending.

4. H — 60
   A — 140   Alf + 80 (Maximum score 30)

Alf pulled the stops out and got an overwhelming difference of 80 points. This introduces an important counter-balancing rule — *the maximum gain on any one play is 30 yards.* (The goal kick is not considered as a 'play' as only one side is doing the kicking.)
Alf's impressive throw (and about time) moves the ball the maximum 30 yards and for the first time in the game he has gone into the attack.
The ball has soared across mid-field and onto Harvey's 25 yard line.
This gives Alf a shot at the double bull for a possible goal. Steady Alf . . . Zonk, into the 8's.
Alf misses and the ball is moved forward 8 yards and Harvey has possession.
5th play.

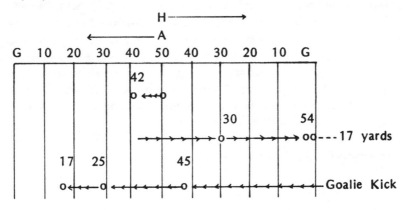

Harvey throws first and scores a 45.
Alf follows with a 60.
Alf has regained possession and moved the ball 15 yards to the 2 yard line from where he can again throw one dart for a goal. As he has passed the 21 yard line any place in the bull counts.
Alf makes no mistake about this one as he sinks his dart smartly into the button. He is one up.

116

After a goal is scored the ball is brought back to the mid-field line, where play is resumed. It is Harvey's ball since his opponent just scored.

He throws a 60. Alf, still jubilant from his goal, gets a 95. The maximum rule applies again and Alf moves the ball 30 yards to the 20 yard line. He is again in position for another shot at goal, one dart any bull.

He throws too hastily and slips into the single 20. The ball is moved 20 yards to the goal line. (Note that the goal line is still in play).

This action brings the board to the present state:

5.   H − 45   A + 15
     A − 60

6.   H − 60   (A + 35) Max 30
     A − 95

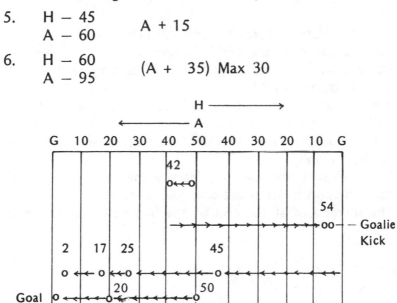

Since Alf missed his shot for goal Harvey takes over on his own goal line. He begins the 7th play with a 95. Alf throws an even 100. Since Harvey began the play with possession of the ball and Alf outscored him, Harvey has pushed the ball over his own goal line and therefore Alf qualifies for a corner kick.

A corner kick is a toughy. Alf must throw one dart for any double. If he gets a double, then he can throw for a goal, (single or double bull). If Alf misses the double or the bull, the ball is placed on the 20 yard line with

Harvey taking possession for the next play.

Alf throws for a double, and does indeed miss. So the 8th play starts with the ball at Harvey's feet on his 20 yard line.

Both players score 100.

The rule that applies here is that the one in possession of the ball when there's a tie score moves the ball 5 yards towards his opponent's goal.

The ball goes to the 25 yard line with Harvey still in possession for the start of the 9th play. (Remember, because Harvey has possession Alf cannot take a kick for goal.)

9th play. Harvey scores 85, and Alf 60.

The ball moves to the mid-field line.

Harvey, with the ball, opens the 10th play with a 100 and Alf throws an 80.

Harvey has now moved the ball up to Alf's 30 yard line. With half-time looming up and the crowd roaring Harvey has one quick chance to even things up by scoring a goal on double bull.

Loud whistles and catcalls, Harvey misses, and the first half closes with Alf ahead one goal to nil.

The scoreboard at the end of the first half would read as follows:

1. H — 52   A + 8
    A — 60

2. A — 55   H + 28   Goalie Kicks
    H — 83   A   H
                                            45 yards|
3. A — .45   H + 1
    H — 46

4. H — 60   A + 80   A + 30 MAX
    A — 140

5. H — 45   A + 15   Corner Kicks
    A — 60   A   H
                                            MISS |
6. H — 60   A + 35   A + 30 MAX
    A — 95

7. H — 95
   A — 100   A + 5

8. H — 100
   A — 100   H + 5 (POSSESSION)

9. H — 85
   A — 60   H + 25

10. H — 100
    A — 80   H + 20

Goal Shots

A	H
MISS	MISS
GOAL	MISS
MISS	MISS

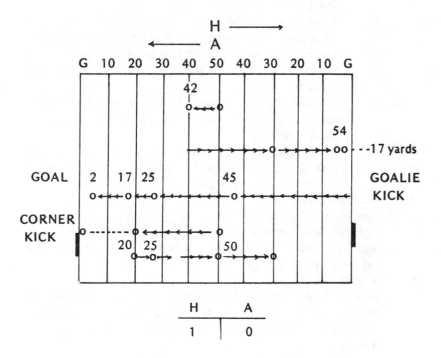

H	A
1	0

• Summary of Rules

For those readers still floundering on the thirty yard line, we provide the following re-cap of the rules to the game of Soccadarts.

* **Starting**

  Middle-for diddle for ball possession. Roles reverse at start of second half.
* **Possession**
  a)   Earned by the higher-scoring player.
  b)   Determines who throws first in each play.
  c)   Qualifies a player for goal attempts, goal kicks and corner kicks.
* **Goal attempts**
  a)   A player having possession of the ball *on or between his opponents 30 and 21 yard line* may throw one dart for a double bull to score a goal.
  b)   A player having possession of the ball *on or between his opponents 20 yard and goal line* may throw one dart for a single or double bull to score a goal.
  c)   All goals valued at one point. A double bull does *not* count for two points.
  d)   If a goal attempt misses, the ball moves the distance equal to the dart's score and possession is given to the defending player.
  e)   If the goal attempt misses and the number scored puts the ball beyond the goal line the defending player qualifies for a goal kick.
* **Length of Game**

  The standard game consists of 20 plays, ten per half. Time out for light refreshments is allowed at half-time. The length of play is, of course variable, depending on the calibre of the players.
* **A Play**

  A play is one throw (three darts) for each player. The objective of the throw is to try and outscore the opponent. Doubles and trebles count their respective values.
* **Yardage**

  The yardage the ball moves is equal to the difference between the players' scores in one play. The high scorer moves the ball the appropriate distance towards his opponent's goal. The maximum yardage allowed from one play is 30 yards. In the case of equal play scores the possessor of the ball gains 5 yards.
* **Goal Kick**
  a)   Anytime the ball is put beyond the opponent's goal line by a player in possession a goal kick is called.
  b)   A goal kick is three darts. Their accumulated score is the yardage the ball is moved from the goal line.

Possession is then given to the opposing player.

* Corner Kick

a) If a player in possession of the ball is forced back across his own goal line the opponent then qualifies for a corner kick.

b) A corner kick is made by throwing one dart at any double. If the double is hit, the player can then make a goal attempt — either the single or double bull in one dart.

c) If either the double or the bull is missed the ball is placed on the defender's 20 yard line with the defender in possession.

Goal attempts, goal kicks and corner kicks are not recorded as 'play' throws.

Double Down (DDD***)

Every player is on his own and there's no limit to the number participating.

In this game every player is competing against all other contestants. It is an ideal game when there's an odd assortment of people (or an assortment of odd people) waiting for a game and it is difficult to form teams without relegating somebody to the sidelines.

● To start.

Nearest the middle, alphabetical order, tallest, shortest, hairiest ... whatever you like, as it does not make a great deal of difference to the final outcome.

Mark the scoreboard with everybody's initial(s). The order for the second and subsequent games can be established by the results of the previous game, the lowest score going first.

Let's put the two old battlers Harvey and Alf back on the mat. Harvey starts first as he is the hairiest.

		15	16	D	17	18	T	19	20	B	Total
H	40										
A	40										

D-Doubles, T-Trebles, B-Bull

121

Each player is given 40 points to start the game. Harvey throws all three darts for 15's. His objective is to score as many 15's as possible. Double and trebles are worth their usual values.

If no fifteens at all are hit his starting total of 40 is reduced by half to 20.

But Harvey isn't the kind to miss 15's.

He throws two singles and a treble to open with a score of 75. This 75 goes on top of his starting gift of 40. Alf throws three single 15's — total 45, so the table is marked:

		15	16	D	17	18	T	19	20	B	Total
H	40	115									
A	40	85									

Scores are accumulated after each throw.

● **Next throw.**

		15	16	D	17	18	T	19	20	B	Total
H	40	115	179								
A	40	85	149								

Harvey gets two single 16's and a double 16. — total 64. Alf throws a single 16, treble 16 and a miss — total 64.

		15	16	D	17	18	T	19	20	B	Total
H	40	115	179	219							
A	40	85	149	75							

Harvey — two misses and a double 20. — total 40.

Alf — misses a double with all three darts, therefore his score is halved.

Note: *Anytime a target is missed with the complete throw the player's accumulated total is cut in half, as was Alf's in the last throw.*

The player is given the benefit of the half point when dividing an odd number in two.

122

● **Next throw**

		15	16	D	17	18	T	19	20	B	Total
H	40	115	179	219	110						
A	40	85	149	75	143						

Harvey hits the wire twice and misses the 17's with his last dart. Rotten luck. His nice big total is chopped in two. Alf comes back into contention with a treble 17 and a single 17 — total 68.

		15	16	D	17	18	T	19	20	B	Total
H	40	115	179	219	110	236					
A	40	85	149	75	143	233					

Harvey — two treble 18's and a single 18 — 126. Good arrows!

Alf — a treble 18 and two singles — 90.

		15	16	D	17	18	T	19	20	B	Total
H	40	115	179	219	110	236	296				
A	40	85	149	75	143	233	308				

Harvey gets a treble 20 and two misses — total 60
Alf hits a treble 15, then a treble 10 and a miss — total 75

		15	16	D	17	18	T	19	20	B	Total
H	40	115	179	219	110	236	296	391			
A	40	85	149	75	143	233	308	365			

Harvey — treble 19 and two single 19's for 95.
Alf — three single 19's — 57

		15	16	D	17	18	T	19	20	B	Total
H	40	115	179	219	110	236	296	391	471		
A	40	85	149	75	143	233	308	365	465		

Harvey — treble 20 single 20 and a bad lob into the backboard. — total 80.

Alf — very cool, a treble 20 and two single 20's for a timely ton.

		15	16	D	17	18	T	19	20	B	Total
H	40	115	179	219	110	236	296	391	471	546	546
A	40	85	149	75	143	233	308	365	465	233	233

● **The Bullfight.**

Harvey zaps one into the bunghole for 50, and a single bull for 25.

Alf crumbles under the pressure and misses the bull with all three arrows.

Harvey wins a very tight game.

Just for the record

The maximum score possible in this game is 1465 — if there's anybody ever done it we would like his autograph. And beginners, don't worry about being whitewashed, the lowest possible score is 1.

English Cricket (DDD****)

Can be played by two players or teams.

This dart version of cricket closely follows the real game; is not vulnerable to the weather, only takes a fraction of the time, and isn't as complicated.

One side bats and the other side bowls (pitches).

You can decide which does what by a middle-for-diddle throw.

The scoreboard is marked up like this:

```
            A        H
1.
2.
3.
4.
5.
6.
7.
8.
9.
```

The numbers 1 through 9 represent the wickets (strike-outs) needed by the bowler in order to end the innings of the batsman. Once nine wickets have been captured by the bowler the roles are reversed.

A wicket is hit by throwing a single bull or a double bull (two wickets).

The batsman starts the game. His objective is to score as many runs (points) as possible with his three darts. Doubles and trebles count their respective values.

To make runs he must score more than 40 with his throw. Any score over 40 counts as the number of runs for the batsman. If, for instance, he throws a 20, 20, and a 5 then he would get 5 runs.

If a batsman fails to score at least 41 points with his throw then he scores a 'duck'. He does not lose anything, but then he does not gain anything.

He must keep his prime objective in mind: to get as many runs as possible before the bowler gets all his nine wickets. The batsman may score anywhere on the board except bull. If he hits a bull he loses one of his own wickets.

The perfect bowler is a bull artist. The sole target for his every dart is the bull. The more he hits the faster he wipes out the batsman and the fewer the runs scored against him.

WARNING to the bowler. For throwing any dart outside the treble ring he gets the punishment he deserves. The score hit by that errant dart is automatically put on the score of the batsman.

Round the Clock, or Round the Horn (DDD*)

Version I

Any number of people can play. A good game for the beginner. Each player starts on number 1 with the idea of placing one dart in each segment up to 20, in sequence. The first 20 hit ends the game, or, if the players are feeling ambitious the bull can be used as the game shot. All doubles and trebles on the board count as singles.

Same game, Version II (DDD**)

Players start on any double and then try to place one dart in each section progressively from 1 through to 20. Finishing requires one dart in the bull and one in treble 20. A player who scores on the last dart of his throw can continue to throw another three darts.

Same game, Version III (DDD***)

Start on a double 1 then place a dart in each section from 2 to 19. Finish off with a double 20, bull and treble 20. Every time a player scores with all three darts he qualifies for a further throw.

Same game, Version IV (DDD****)

Getting tough. Players must go around the board from 1 to 20 on doubles and finish on a bull. Again, three scoring darts win the player a free turn.

Same game, Version V (DDD*****)

Any double starts the game and the players must go around the board on trebles. Finish is a double twenty and three double bulls. A player scoring with all three darts gets a free throw.

Round-the-clock games are perfect for practice. They can be used to gradually raise the beginner's level of play. Start with Version 1, recording how many darts it takes to complete the game and then progress onto Version II, and so forth. When you can get around the clock in any one version consistently in 20-25 throws, move up a notch.

Competence in Version IV and V calls for a very high level of marksmanship as it is in the areas of doubles and trebles where darts trophies are won.

Just for the record

Jim Pike's Round-the-Clock on doubles in 3½ minutes stood as a world record for 34 years; it has only recently been topped.

Shanghai (DDD*)

For any number of players. Each player progresses around the clock from 1 through 20. At each number he throws three darts. The aim is to score as many points as possible in each segment with three darts, doubles and trebles counting. The highest accumulated score at the completion of all twenty segments decides the winner.

Just for the record

The maximum score possible in this game of Shanghai is 1890.

Shanghai Version II (DDD**)

Any number can play. Only the numbers 1 to 7 are used. All three darts are thrown at each number in turn and the highest possible score amassed. Doubles and trebles count their usual values. The top score after seven throws is the winner.

There are three hazards to make things more interesting. The 'Shang,' the 'Hai' and the "Shanghai".

The Shang. This is any one of the numbers (usually a 3) designated prior to play. Missing this number with all three darts means the player's score at that stage is reduced to 0.

The Hai. This is the 5's. Missing the 5's with all three darts sends the player back to his beer, he's out of luck and out of the game.

The Shanghai. This is a bonanza for the player who gets it and a tragedy for the other players. Shanghai is, in one throw, hitting a single, double and treble of any of the numbers in the game. This feat wins the game there and then and no further darts can be thrown.

Argument on whether the single, double and treble should be hit in that or any other order has rocked the darts capitals of the world for generations. A generally accepted rule is that the single must not be the last dart to go in.

Just for the record

Highest score possible is 252 (a realistic average is around 80).

Scram (DDD*)

Played by two players or teams. Middle-for-diddle starts the game. The closest to the bull has the choice of being a 'Stopper' or a 'Scorer' for the first half of the game.

In the second half the roles are reversed. Doubles and trebles count, and bulls are not used in the game.

1		
2		
3		
4		
5		
6		
7		
8		
9		
10		
11		
12		
13		
14		
15		
16		
17		
18		
19		
20		

The Stopper throws first with the object of hitting any number from 1 to 20. The numbers hit by the Stopper are automatically killed for the Scorer. If the Stopper gets a 20, 5, and 19 on his throw these numbers are erased or crossed out, showing they are no longer active. The Scorer can aim for anything and everything except the numbers killed by the Stopper. Every valid number he hits scores its respective number of points. As the game progresses his choice of targets is narrowed down until the Stopper has killed all numbers. It is now the other player's turn to try and beat his opponents score. Note that the darts can be poured into any one segment as often as wished until that number is killed.

Shove Ha' Penny (DDD**)

For any number of players. This is a dart adaptation of the true pub game. Only the numbers 1 to 9 are used, with singles worth one point, doubles worth two and trebles three points. Each player can throw at any of the nine numbers. If a player scores more than three points in any one number the excess points are given to the next player down, or the player on the board needing the points to fill in that score segment.

The idea is to fill in every 3-point-box the fastest possible. Ideally it can be done in three throws with nine trebles. Not much subtlety required for this game, merely a hit or miss affair.

Take a quick look at a game that Harvey and Alf have just started.

	1	2	3	4	5	6	7	8	9
A	III	I							
H	I								

Alf hit four 1's and a single 2. As he got more 1's than required he donates one to a grateful Harvey.

When Harvey throws he will need two single 1's (or one double) to complete his 1's box.

Remember, boxes may be filled in any order.

The first player to fill all nine boxes first is declared the winner. The winning shot, however, must be scored, not received from an opponent.

All Fives (DDD****)

Any number can play. A good fast game at which it is easy to win (or lose) a few pints. Seems straightforward enough but requires some quick thinking, nerves of steel, and a close familiarity with the board.

If you are not too fast with the figurework you could lose your shirt.

All numbers on the board are used, including trebles, doubles and bulls.

The winner is the first player to score fifty-one 'Fives'.

With each throw a player has to score a number which is divisible by 5. Every 'Five' he gets is one point. For example 20, 20 and 5 = 45 = 9 points (5 x 9 = 45) One Ton (100) is 20 points. If the total score from three darts cannot be divided by 5 the throw is wasted.

The last dart of a throw must be in a scoring bed. If a third dart misses the numbers or falls out the throw earns no points, even if the first two darts score a multiple of 5. In finishing the game all three darts must be used and a player must hit the exact score required to gain his fifty-one 'fives'. The scoreboard can be marked up either way, with every player starting with fifty-one points, or the fifty-one can be accumulated.

Note: *The 15/10 'pie' is a relatively safe scoring area.*

Dominoes (DDD**)

Another highly interesting game, this one closely following the pub game of dominoes.

It is so close to the real game in fact that you need a set of dominoes to play it, and some darts, of course.

First of all, share 28 dominoes out equally between each player. Only the numbers 1 through 6 are used on the board. Each player looks at his own dominoes. The first one off exposes a domino and has to hit its corresponding number on the board (with a dart, not a domino). For instance, if the turned domino shows a 6/3, he must also hit a single 6 and 3 on the dartboard.

The next player requires a domino with a 3 or 6 to lay along the one already down. If he has one he exposes it and throws to hit the corresponding numbers on the board. If he doesn't have the required domino he 'knocks' — (misses his turn). Any player missing the numbers on the board with any of his 3 darts also has to 'knock'. The first player to get rid of all his dominoes is the winner. A blank domino requires throwing between the double ring and the outer edge of the board.

To play a double (for example, 4/4) a player must hit the double 4. If all three darts miss he 'knocks' and retrieves his domino.

Grand National (Horse Racing)   (DDD****)

Individual participation, no limit on numbers.
As with horse racing, one of the major attractions of the game is wagering, mostly with a pot.
The object is to jump all the fences and complete the circuit first.
Most beginners will not be able to complete the course.
It consists of only the inner parts of the single segments (i.e. between the bull and the treble ring) and the following trebles, 13, 17, 8 and 5.
The course is laid out as follows: (Remember all singles are inners).

Singles	20
	1
	18
	4
Treble	13 (first fence)
Singles	6
	10
	15
Two Treble	17's (second fence)
Singles	3
	19
	7
	16
Treble	8 (third fence)
Singles	11
	14
	9
	12
Treble	5 (fourth fence)
Any Bull	(finishing line).

What makes the game tough and the fences a hazard is that each player is only allowed three throws (nine darts) at each number. Failure to hit the number in the required darts will be a fallen horse and the player will be out of the race.

The exceptions are:

Treble 17   — two treble 17's are required therefore 6 throws are allowed.

Bull   — You can throw for the finish until the bar closes.

Handicaps may be given for the race that allow players to either start further down the field, or give them an extra throw per fence. But it is well to remember a poor starter may easily win if the horses ahead of him fall at the fences.

Golf (DDD***)

A very close simulation of the actual game with all the scoring patterns and frustrations. Excellent game for old golfers.

The object is, of course, to go round 18 holes with the intention of beating par and your opposition. Par score is 54, which works out at par three for each hole.

The numbers 1 through 18 are used with each number representing a hole. Three darts in a hole, (which are played sequentially) moves the player onto the next hole. Since doubles and trebles count, hitting a treble of a number would be equal to a hole-in-one and a double/single would be a birdie. The scorecard registers the number of darts thrown for each hole.

Each 'golfer' keeps throwing until he 'holes-out', i.e. gets three hits.

If a treble is hit with the first arrow the player can either sit down and take the hole-in-one as his throw or move onto the next hole with his remaining two darts. Handicaps are easy to apply using the same procedure as with that other game played on grass.

Car Rallying (DDD***)

Each player is on his own in this one and any number can play, within reasonable limits.

Before starting play a specific rally route has to be laid out on the scoreboard. Along the route obstacles are set up. The route may be any length, all 20 segments of the board if you like, with obstacles at any position.

Here's a sample route:

Single	1
Inner	1
Double	1
Treble	1
Inner	20
Outer	20
Obstacle (two treble 20's)	

Obstacles usually comprise hitting a tough number twice before continuing on the circuit. As you can see, the route may be made as difficult or easy as you wish and can wander all across the face of the board.

However, the finishing line is always on the bull, which requires two hits to finish.

English Football (Soccer)

Version II (DDD****)

Can be played by two players or teams.

Rule-wise the game is a cinch, especially when compared to the multi-rule Soccadarts game described earlier. Play-wise it can be a brute of a game as only doubles and bulls count.

The starter is the player winning the middle-for-diddle throw. The first objective is to get possession of the ball. This is done by throwing a bull. Once a player has hit a bull he can make a goal attempt. A goal is scored simply by hitting any double. If a bull is hit with the player's first dart he has the chance of getting two doubles with the next two darts. Each double hit counts as one goal.

The nasty aspect of the game is for the poor fellow who can't hit a bull. The player in possession can keep scoring on doubles until the ball is taken away from him by his opponent hitting a bull. The roles then switch.

The first player to score ten goals is the winner.

Round-the-Clock Version VI (DDD***)

This version of round-the-clock should present most

competitive enjoyment to a group of semi-skilled players. It is possible, with a perfect throw to tie up the whole game in just eight darts.

On the other hand, the same semi-skilled player on an off-night can stagger to a tortuous sixty-dart finish if all he can manage is one number with three darts.

The principle of the game is the same as other round-the-clock versions. The difference is that the doubles count as their usual values (though not the trebles) and hitting, say, a double 3, jumps the player to the next number — 7, (double three counting as a six). The experts can therefore 'run' around the board with a few well-chosen doubles, while the duffers hitting singles have to 'walk' around.

The perfect throw would be:

1.	Double	1
2.	Single	3
3.	Double	4
4.	Single	9
5.	Double	10

The finish is a repeat of the first double hit and its treble and a bull, so,

6.	Double	1
7.	Treble	1
8.	Bull	

Consider a lousy throw. All it needs is to miss doubles where it is most important to hit them.

Single	1, 2
Double	3 (lucky shot)
Single	7, 8, 9, 10, 11, 12, 13, 14, 15, 16, 17, 18, 19, 20.

Missing the double ten means a long hike through all the singles to 20 as double values overscore from 10 upwards. This would take at least ten darts. Finishing in this case would be a double 3, treble 3 and a bull. If no doubles are hit in the first ten numbers the player has to finish on double 1, treble 1 and bull.

English Rounders (DDD***)

Played by two players or partners. This is a clever dart adaptation of the game that the English claim is the predecessor to baseball. The only areas of the board used are the segments 1 through 9 representing the innings that are played sequentially. Also the bull is active (single and double).

A treble is a three base hit, a double a two base hit, and a single a one base hit. The bull counts as a four base hit, double bull allows a bonus run.

Two players: Winner of the middle-for-diddle throw has the choice of batting first or second. The first player up must throw two darts at the one (first inning). On his *third* dart (and only on his third dart), he has the choice of throwing for a home run (bull) or for the ones again. If for example Harvey bats first and throws a double one, a single one (this single moves the second base runner to third), and then another single one, he has scored one run with runners left on first and second base.

Alternatively, after having thrown the double one and single one with two darts, a confident player could try for a bull with his last dart. A single bull would have scored a total of three runs.

A double bull would give three runs plus a bonus run. Following Harvey's throw it is Alf's turn at batting for score in the 1st box.

The score is kept with the same lay-out as regular baseball.

Baseball Innings

	1	2	3	4	5	6	7	8	9
H									
A									

If the score is tied at the end of regulation play, extra innings can be added to establish a winner.

Partners

The same basic rules apply throughout the game for partners, with the following exceptions:

*   The two partners on each team throw their darts in succession so one inning will be a six-dart throw per team.
*   Only the last dart thrown of the six can be aimed for a home run.

Naughts an' Crosses (TIC, TAC, TOE) (DDD****)

Slightly more difficult than the actual game played on paper.

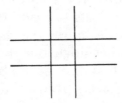

After marking the board as shown, the game gets tough. The object, of course, is to gain a straight line through any three sectors with X's or O's before your opponent does.

This straight line through the sectors must always be composed of a double of any number, a bull and a double of the number *directly opposite* the other double on the clock. (If one double is a 5, then the other double must be a 17 — or if one double is a 20 then the other double must be a 3. It must be emphasized that the bull must always be the TAC (Center) of the Tic, Tac, Toe.

So if Harvey wins the honors of starting the game from Alf, he has the choice of taking X's or O's. Harvey likes the big O's and proceeds to throw his first round.

On his first dart, he hits a bull and must now stop a second to consider his strategy. (Since the bull must always be the Tac of Tic Tac Toe, Harvey must decide where he wants to place his first X representing the bull. He has five choices which are shown as follows:

```
        | B |
   _____|___|_____
    B | B | B
   ‾‾‾‾‾|‾‾‾|‾‾‾‾‾
        | B |
        |   |
```

Harvey mentally decides on placing his X in the middle box and proceeds to throw his remaining two darts. He hits a double 20 with his second and misses the double 3 with the third. The board is now marked up as follows. (Note: the 3 is directly opposite the 20 on the board.)

```
   X |   |                    20 |   |
  ___|___|___                ____|___|___
     | X |                       | B |
  ‾‾‾|‾‾‾|‾‾‾                ‾‾‾‾|‾‾‾|‾‾‾
     |   |                       |   |
```

Alf has a choice of trying to stop Harvey's Tic, Tac, Toe by scoring any double and placing his in the bottom right hand corner. He does so by hitting a double 11 and he then throws a miss and a bull. He marks his score as follows:

```
   X |   |                    20 |   |
  ___|___|___                ____|___|___
     | X | O                     | B | B
  ‾‾‾|‾‾‾|‾‾‾                ‾‾‾‾|‾‾‾|‾‾‾
     | O |                       |   | 11
```

Harvey toes the line and throws a double 3 which he puts in the top right hand corner to stop Alf and then throws a bull to win the game for himself.

```
   X | X | X                  20 | B | 3
  ___|___|___                ____|___|___
     | X | O                     | B | B
  ‾‾‾|‾‾‾|‾‾‾                ‾‾‾‾|‾‾‾|‾‾‾
     | O |                       |   | 11
```

Alternatively, he could have hit any double to stop Alf and then thrown its opposite number for across down in the bottom left section to win.

CHAPTER IX

The Darts Team

It doesn't take long for a group of darts regulars at a local watering hole to get together and start talking about spreading their wings beyond their own domain. Once a player gets hooked on the game he invariably plays and plays until he reaches a level of competence that he feels must be exposed to the cold draughts of alien opposition. Playing among friends is fun but when it comes to flexing one's darts muscles he must enter into the big wide world beyond the local tavern.

Too often a player becomes stagnated within his own darts sphere and, although capable of caning his friends regularly, reaches a plateau of play that may be pleasant but not progressive.

Succeeding outside the warmth of one's own environment against unknown players of unknown skill is the experience that molds the future champions.

Not every individual wants to wander alone from pub to pub turning over every stone in the hopes of finding a worthy opponent on whom to test his dartability. It would be a hit and miss affair and doesn't help create the right atmosphere in which darts is intended to be played. This is a game of skill, certainly, but more important it is a game to be enjoyed with friends.

The National Darts Association of Great Britain has decided that the definition of a professional is one whose main source of income comes from the game. Therefore winning the odd large monetary prize doesn't mean a loss of amateur status.

The answer is the darts team.

Forming a team is simple; maintaining its direction and cohesion is tough. The key to unlock the potential of a good team is a combination of both players' abilities and sound management.

The good manager, ideally a rusty old player knowing all the angles, is a strong individual endowed with a dynamic personality and matching energy, a surplus of business acumen and a wife with a generous nature.

His responsibilities include, but are not limited to:

Inception

*   Selecting team members and reserves.
*   Hunting down a well-heeled sponsor (one who will benefit from the team's successes or patronage).
*   Obtaining a venue for home matches.
    If the sponsor is the owner of a bar the venue should present no problem.
*   Establishing contact with the local darts association. If no local association exists, then start one.
*   Ironing out the throwing problems of the weaker members of the team.

Match preparation

*   Coaching (usually frowned upon). Simply make sure every member has a copy of this book.
*   Working out game strategy, captains, alloting throwing order (experts on doubles, bulls, etc.)
*   Mapping out match games, rules, stakes, etc. With rival team manager.
*   Arranging travel accommodations for away games. Making sure everybody arrives on time. Placating wives and/or girlfriends of team members.
*   Arranging the victuals on home matches (could be delegated to a sub-committee).

Actual Match

*   Shaking hands with rival manager.
*   Restraining team from trying to drain out contents

"He's useless on doubles"

of opponent's bar prior to the match.
* Dragging team from opposition's wives and/or girl-friends.
* Organizing actual games, throwing and scorekeeping sequence.
* Making friends and understanding problems of rival manager over a quiet drink.
* Making sure a good percentage of the team arrives back in their home town.

Post Match

* Calling up wives and/or girlfriends to explain late or non-arrival home of certain players.
* Contacting lawyers, arranging bail for wayward players in distant lock-ups.
* Posting a copy of this book to rival manager.
* Recruiting new members to fill the gaps in the team's ranks.

Yes, it is a big job and a heavy responsibility, so it may be best if we offer some hints for the manager-to-be. Perhaps the most important area is the selection of team members. You cannot afford to do this haphazardly. It takes care, patience and understanding. The wise manager enrolls in a night course in psychology at the local university.

The following may serve as a guide in the selection of the perfect team, but then again, it may not.

Guide to Darts Team Member Selection

Merits	Far exceeds team requirements	Exceeds team requirements	Meets team requirements	Acceptable based on lack of candidates	Does not meet team requirements
Adaptability	Walks on water	Keeps head above water under stress	Sometimes washes with water	Drinks water	Passes water under stress
Gregarious-ness	Talks with God	Talks with the angels	Talks to himself	Argues with himself	Loses argument with himself
Promptness	Arrives two days ahead of match	Arrives in time for match	Arrives in time to par-take in the "Gallon" of match	Arrives wrong place for match	Burns fingers on match
Physical attributes	Stronger than a bull	Shoots the bull	Can almost see the bull	Looks like a bull	Smells like a bull
Confidence	Thinks he's Robin Hood	Thinks he's Errol Flynn	Wishes he was someone else	Doesn't care who he is	Doesn't know who. he is

Another method of selection would involve actual dart throwing ability. For this system of selection the house darts ladder is a valuable help. If it is a 12-member ladder the top 8 would compose the team and the bottom four the reserves for that particular match. Climbing into the top eight of the ladder would automatically qualify a player for a position in the match team.

A new, and more sophisticated, method is to establish a handicap system which classifies all potential team members into specific categories based on their marksmanship.

In England, for example, a new national handicapping system has been developed called the National Darts Register.

To establish a handicap the player obtains a special printed card which is filled out according to the player's throw. The card is signed by two witnesses. Three completed cards are necessary to work out the playing handicap and no two cards can be completed within the same week. It works like this:

Each card lists the numbers 1 through 20 and the player has one throw at each number in sequence, starting with the 1's and finishing on 20's. Doubles and trebles are recorded as singles and only the number of darts hitting each sector are counted.

After three such cards are completed the scores are added together and divided by three. The resulting average is deducted from sixty (which represents the maximum of three darts in each of the twenty sectors). The final figure is the player's handicap.

Sector Number	Score
1	2
2	2
3	1
4	3
5	1
6	3
7	1
8	3
9	3
10	3

11	3
12	1
13	1
14	3
15	2
16	1
17	2
18	0
19	2
20	1
Total	38

For instance, if a player throws 38 the first time and then a 43 and a 45, his handicap would be as follows:

38 + 43 + 45 = 126

Divided by 3 = 42

Subtracted from 60 = 18 Handicap

Players in the National Darts Register are graded according to their handicaps:

Grand Master	0 – 3
Master	4 – 7
Expert	8 – 11
Marksman	12 – 15
Leagueman	16 – 20
Standard	20 – 25

This is the original D. J. Crawley handicapping system which he has since vastly improved. The handicaps are now secretly calculated by experts with a claim that it is 99.9 percent flawless. Players wishing to establish their handicap may try writing directly to National Darts Register, 26 Orchard Piece, Blackmore, Ingatestore, Essex, England.

So there we are.

Maybe it is worth noting that all handicapping systems to date have excluded one influence common to the majority of players .... wives. Bachelors may appear to be the logical choice for the heavily booked team but the married man, once he has decided where his loyalties lie can add stability, wisdom and experience to a team. Selecting the right kind of married man calls for an extension to the normal handicapping system to include, besides the usual ingredients of good company, moral character, keg capacity and dartability, the important asset of availability. And this is where wives come into the picture.

Do not be too keen to enroll on the team the fellow who dominates the board every Friday night. If he only ever comes into the pub on Fridays it is a safe bet he is only allowed out once a week. And though he may be all too willing to accept the honor of team membership you may be in for a disappointment if you expect to see him turn up for every match.

So look for availability, particularly with married men and remember the biggest handicap is often a wife. Perhaps inviting wives along for a darts social evening may help the team captain smooth the way for henpecked husbands.

Handicaps (not wives) can also help in arranging the team's fixtures. There is no point in travelling three hundred miles to play a team whose top players are obviously well below the standard of your own team.

A pub in Peterborough, England, has a resident darts team called 'The United Nations'. Players of thirteen nations comprise the team: two Germans, a Hungrian, two Chinese, a Malayan, a Pakistani, a West Indian, an Irish, a Welshman, an Icelander, a Canadian, an Italian, a Ukranian and, yes, an American.
What, no English?

Once a team for a match is chosen it is a good idea to insist on one or two reserves actually coming along for the match. Do not rely on a last minute telephone call to reserves. Turning up at a match with too many players gives an advantage the clever captain can use to devastating effect on the opposition.

Standing on a stool or table, in a loud voice he pretends to select the team (which was actually chosen a week ago).

"Alf, you've got the East Coast Finals coming up on Saturday so I'd like you to step down tonight and take it easy. Fred, if you could take his place and remember to leave Harvey on the double tops . . . and you, Jerry, go to number three position tonight and don't let last week's seven dart finish go to your head . . ." etcetera.

On the other side of the coin there is nothing worse than arriving at a far-off tavern to find your best two players have gone to the wrong pub, been booked for speeding, or got stuck in a snowdrift. Plan to have more than enough players. It is experience for junior members of the team and they will get a chance to play with some of the opposition in friendly games after the match. The reserves who turn up and do not get a chance to play in the match should automatically be on the team in the next fixture.

Internal competition within the club for team places is no bad thing. A player who takes for granted his place on the team may get careless and not pull out all the stops at the right time. If each member of the team values his position the manager will always have an excess of good players.

What is the best number for a team?

This varies, mainly on the arrangements made with the rival team. League teams usually have a set standard. Since regular matches will be termed 'friendly', teams should allow for as many players as practical to participate without the match dragging on into the night. Six, seven, eight or nine players per team make for a good match but eight players is the ideal size.

With eight players to a team try the following match program.

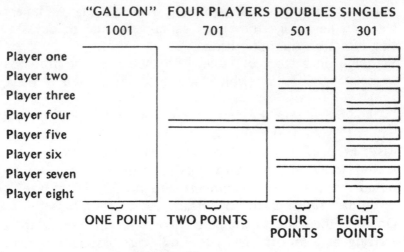

	"GALLON"	FOUR PLAYERS	DOUBLES	SINGLES
	1001	701	501	301

Player one
Player two
Player three
Player four
Player five
Player six
Player seven
Player eight

ONE POINT   TWO POINTS   FOUR POINTS   EIGHT POINTS

TOTAL POINTS: 15

The "gallon" is always one game of 1001, straight start, double finish with all players playing in order. The games of 701, 501, and 301 can be one or three legs per game.

Seven Players/Team Play:

Total points for the match would be eleven.

*	The "gallon", one game 1001	— 1 point
*	Three games 301, best out of three legs, by partners	— 3 points
*	Seven games 301, best out of three legs, individual	— 7 points
		11 points

NOTE: *One member of each team will have to stand down for the partners games.*

148

Nine Players/Team Play:

Total points for the match would be seventeen.

*	The "gallon", one game 1001	— 1 point
*	Three games 701, three players to a side, one leg	— 3 points
*	Four games 501, best out of three legs, partners	— 4 points
*	Nine games 301, one leg	— 9 points
		17 points

NOTE: *One member of each team stands down for the partners game.*

The game sequence can be decided by the managers before play. Some prefer to have the 'gallon' played first, others prefer it to be last, as in a close match the one point it earns can be the decider and the end of the match can be an exciting affair. The 'gallon' is also the drink winner for every member of the team so it also adds a touch of bonhomie to the final.

Arranging the individual team order of play can be a ticklish job for the manager. Each should know the capabilities of each member of the team, their strengths and weaknesses. The following team order has proved successful:

1. Best player
2. Fifth best player
3. Other
4. Other
5. Third best player
6. Other
7. Fourth best player
8. Second best player

If the team disgraces itself on the board, well, the manager can chalk it up to experience. But if the team disgraces itself off the board the manager better be prepared to cover his embarassment. The following form, to be filled out by the offending players and handed to the rival manager, may help save the situation.

Mr. _____

Regrets exceedingly his deplorable conduct while a guest at your pub on _____ and begs your forgiveness for the breach of etiquette as checked below.

☐ Spilling drink
☐ Hitting host with bottle
☐ Complete loss of equilibrium
☐ Passing out
☐ Failing to zip pants
☐ Taking off pants
☐ Gut rumbling (above 60 Db)
☐ Failing to properly identify bathroom fixtures
☐ Mistaking darts trophy as bathroom fixture
☐ Taking home bathroom fixtures
☐ Re-cycling used beer
Others. _____
_____
_____

Once local teams have got themselves organized the next move is to establish a league. This is best done with the assistance of a darts association. Very much the same as is being done with the multitude of bowling leagues throughout the United States.

Anybody with any experience in league work will know its smooth function needs a considerable amount of co-operation and hard work. Each team should select a league representative who will work within a governing body to draw up the rules of play, make fixture schedules and a points system, and obtain a league sponsor or somehow raise funds to support large competitions.

Rules of Play

*   A standard throwing distance may have to be established.
*   A games system drawn up to constitute a match.
*   The number of players per match designated.
*   Teams and players registered, including reserves.
*   Rules formed to govern scorekeeping, refereeing, records. (Team secretaries should also keep records, also each player should fill in his game results card – similar to a golf score card.)
*   Rules made for infractions.

Fixture Schedule

*   Scheduling contests that allow for a fair exchange of 'home' and 'away' games for each team.
*   Establishing the exact number of games to be played for that season.
*   Recording and properly notifying all league members of weekly results and league standings.
*   Publishing (if possible) league tables and news in local press.
*   Recording significant play and forming a local ladder for individual players with an appropriate trophy. (For example, a point can be given for every ton scored, or two points for scores over 170.)
*   Arranging year end play-offs, grand finals, exhibition games, publicity for the game, charity matches, etc.
*   Making a points system for wins, losses and ties. (Provision in scoring is often not made for a tie, but tied games can add extra interest to league standings.)

Sponsors

It can cost very little to run a successful darts team and, fortunately, at this stage of the game sponsorship is not a major problem. All the team requires is a regular venue, enough funds to cover the costs of transportation for away games and enough money in the kitty to provide the opposition with a free round of drinks and something to chew on at home games.

At team level, therefore, a sponsor such as a landlord or club is a handy thing to have for putting the team on a firm playing foundation, but is not essential.

At team level the sponsor would probably derive more benefit from the team's activities than the team would from the sponsor's moral and monetary support.

For support of a team the sponsor would:

a)   gain a hard-core of regular customers — players, hopeful players and supporters,

b)   win publicity for the establishment (presumably the team would adopt the tavern's name so any published team standings would provide free advertising),

c)   make his place a magnet for any darts players in, or moving into, the area,

d)   earn extra revenue from visiting teams.

> A pub called The Castle in South London has a darts room 100 feet long with twelve boards.
> **Ever tried throwing a dart 100 feet?**

In return, the team sponsor would be put to very minor financial outlay. Basically he should:

a)   provide a darts home for the team complete with a good playing area and a well-kept board and sundries,

b)   make sure the team has at least one night's sole use of the board, and perhaps another night for practice.
c)   have made and keep up-to-date a darts ladder (not necessarily for just the team but for all the pub's players.)
d)   pay for a pub trophy for the season's best performance on the team.

And encourage the game in different ways, such as buying a landlord's pint for scorers of 180 and other impressive feats. The good team sponsor can derive unlimited benefits from his team, the better the environment he provides the more likely the team is going to be better organized and play better. With every success of the team the sponsor will glean promotion for his establishment.

Sweden, where every good suana has a dartboard, now has a beer named DART, with a picture of a board on the label.

In the near future the pub without a darts team is going to be a loser. The darts team without a sponsor, is however not such a serious matter. With a following of keen players a team can be set up anywhere and it does not take much initiative to put it on a good financial footing. Some enterprising teams have played and practiced in the backs of garages, donated a weekly subscription, and besides having a healthy bank account have formed the comradeship that makes a well-knit team.

With or without a sponsor it is a good idea for the team treasurer to extract a few cents each week from every member. The accrued cash over a year can really mount up and pay for a team excursion far beyond their normal boundaries. This income is best placed into a high interest savings scheme, not just thrown into an old coffee can, so that team members can, at the end of the season, opt on the percentage to be spent on an excursion or kept in the kitty. It may be more popular to keep the savings accruing interest and to pay out a dividend to every team member at Christmas or Thanksgiving, but the most important factor is that every contributing member knows exactly what they are investing in, how individual and club savings stand, and what plans have been agreed on for whatever amounts are accumulated.

Remember always, the purpose of a team is to play and enjoy the game of darts, not organize a financial institute. So we come to the higher leagues of darts sponsorship. A sponsor for a league is one of the hardest fought after benefactors in the sport. The money spent nowadays on sponsoring tennis, golf, baseball, hockey and numerous other sports is fantastic. Darts has been sadly overlooked by the big sponsors in the past; there are indications this will not be the case in the future.

> The total annual income of darts teams has reached an estimated $30 million in Britain.

Revenue from pubs, breweries, equipment makers, etc. that can directly be attributed to darts players has reached phenomenal proportions on both sides the Atlantic. Unfortunately there seems to be a prevalent attitude amongst the benefactors of the multi-million darts market that the sport either does not need sponsorship, or that it is self-sustaining, or that the returns from investment are negligible.

These arguments hold no water. You can count the number of non-drinking darts players on the vats of one brewery. Income from the game in British pubs is estimated at well over fifty – million dollars a year. For advertisers of beer, spirits and cigarettes the darts world is a compact ready-made market. For these products, what better consumer is there? Football players? Golfers?

Tennis players? Fishermen? ... There has never been a better market created, tailor-made, for sponsorship by certain producers than today's darts millions. And surprisingly, sponsorship of darts requires so little outlay for such tremendous dividends. To sponsor a local league for example the chips are all in the hands of the sponsor. He will:

a)   get direct advertising and mass coverage of every team and player in the league and all their followers,

b)   have his product's name published perhaps as a league name in every report, both local and national on league performance,

c)   associate his name with the people who buy his type of product, associate with local, national and international successes from the league,

d)   cover a tremendously wide group of customers and potential customers,

e)   be part of the growth of the game (as has happened with such boom sports as golf, tennis and bowling),

f)   be able to link his product name with the top players in the league, (many are now heavily booked around the country for exhibition matches) and have priority for sponsorship,

g)   be able to tie in his sponsorship internationally with his sales (note that the American Team won the 1974 US/England match).

For all the advantages that can be gained from league sponsorship the outlay is a drop in the ocean. All that is required of a league sponsor is to:

a)   establish and cover the prize for season-end league championships,

b)   assist in, not necessarily totally support, the expenses of running top tournament matches,

c)   be willing to share in the expenses accrued by league organization during the season.

Another interesting aspect of the sport is that the major sponsor need not be a producer of something imbibed.

*"And a big hand
for the runner-up"*

Britain's, and indeed the world's, major sponsor of championship matches is a newspaper — the 'News of the World'. This venerable newspaper has sponsored national championship games for almost thirty years.

There is presently no equivalent on this side the Atlantic. Perhaps they do not know what is in store for this game. Perhaps the potential sponsor has not been approached in the right manner. Perhaps the sponsor is merely a phone call away, and perhaps the sport is at fault in that it does not realize its own potential. Here are a few facts which you may push under the nose of a man with the means, whether he be a landlord or a national advertiser.

* Over eight million people watched the News of the World International Championship game on television in 1973, in England, that's almost every one-in-six of the population.

* In America, darts players have increased by 300% in the last five years.

* Last year 300,000 players competed for local and national championships.

* The game of darts knows no social, or economic boundaries. Anyone can play!

In 1939, darts hit a peak of popularity in England and a darts tournament staged in the Royal Agricultural Hall in London, matching the great players of London with those of the Southern Countries raised $15,000, winners take all.

A lot of money in 1939.

CHAPTER X

The Relevant and Irrelevant

Life is composed of challenges.
(For many darts players, waking up the morning-after is the biggest challenge of them all.) For the more advanced disciples of the game, however, there are records that shine high above the double 20's. The *Guiness Book of Records* devotes a full page to the accomplishments achieved in significant darts play.

To give enthusiastic types a chance to blazen their names in history, we herewith provide you with the basic qualifications necessary for authentication and insertion in the *Guiness Book of Records*.

Most of the records are established on the basis of time and endurance, and the only way to break these records is to throw faster than the normal recommended pace.

At the same time, reading a record is quite different from actually doing it.

For instance, the record for the most doubles in ten hours is a simple 2,814. That works out to about 4.69 a minute. To a good player, that could be a drop in the bucket. What one should consider, however, is the fact that this 4.69 must be maintained for every minute for *ten hours.*

Consider also the distance that must be covered in retrieving the darts and returning to the hockey: it will exceed *nine miles* — depending on your throwing rate. Most darts players are blessed with an incredible standing up ability, but very rarely a sustained walking ability.

For most Americans, with their school years back in history, covering nine miles on foot is a feat equal to that of Hannibal's.

But if one is still not deterred by the above, and a true record breaker never is, the following conditions must be met by the *Guiness Book of Records*:

Book of Records:

Requirements:

* The accomplishment of the feat should have press coverage in recognized local or national newspaper.
* Recognition of the feat should have signed authentication by an *independent* individual or organization of standing.
* Having broken the record, you will have to repeat the accomplishment if you have not provided a signed log stating that there has been *unremitting* surveillance throughout and that all times and durations are clearly stated — especially those of any rest breaks where applicable.

It should be noted that the *Guiness Book of Records* cannot actually provide personnel for observing record attempts and that they must rely on official governing bodies. In this respect, the governing bodies may have to ratify all activities.

Rest Breaks:

Many of the records already established in darts are in individual marathon tests. In this category, a time allowance of five minutes is allowed for each completed hour. These, of course, are optional. But, as mentioned, they must be recorded in the log. The record for individual marathons is based on total gross time from start to finish. A rest break is not allowable for those tests which are comprised of players or teams. This category must be non-stop without any rest breaks. Sorry.

After you have broken whatever it is you are trying to break, you may have a difficult time in gaining recognition. *Guiness Book of Records* is only likely to recognize marathon records that are significant, such as those that show an improvement on existing records.

They will not recognize records which could be dangerous or injurious to health.

Their objective in accepting a record is based on whether the feat is significant relative to becoming the object of widespread or international competition.

And no cheating! In marathons such as the Million and One, only one board is allowed. One overly intelligent team tried to get around this rule by using both sides of the board by painting the back of the board and hanging it in such a manner so that they could throw at both sides simultaneously. Clever, but hardly cricket.

The greatest feat yet recorded to date is when John Lowe recorded dart history on October 13, 1984, during the televised M.F.I. World Matchplay when he shot the perfect nine dart (180–180–141) 501 game. It was reported that he collected $100,000 for his effort — not to mention the thousands extra for winning most of the events in this prestigious tournament.

The following quotation has been taken from the *Guiness Book of Records**

"LOWEST POSSIBLE SCORES: The lowest number of darts to achieve standard scores are: 201 four darts, 301 six darts, 501 nine darts, 1,001 seventeen darts. The four and six darts "possibles" have been achieved many times, the nine darts 501 occasionally, but never the seventeen darts 1,001 which would require 15 treble 20's, a treble 17 and a 50. The lowest even number which cannot be scored with three darts (ending on a double) is 162. The lowest odd number with cannot be scored with three darts (ending on a double) is 159.

FASTEST MATCH: The record time for going around the board in "doubles" at arm's length is 14.5 seconds by Jim Pike at the Craven Club, Newmarket, in March 1944. The record for this feat at the nine-feet 2.7 meter throwing distance, retrieving own darts, is 2 minutes 13 seconds by Bill Duddy at The Plough, Hornsey Road, Holloway North London on October 18, 1972."

ROUND THE BOARD ON DOUBLES/TEAM MARA-THON: A six man team at the Penwith Social Club, Penzance, Cornwell) went around the board on doubles 89 times in 12 hours. (Mind you, that includes the Bull.)

MILLION AND ONE: On April 4, 1980, a team composed of eight players closed this magic game out in 39,566 darts."

* Published by Guinness Superlatives Limited, 2 Cecil Court, London Road, Enfield, Middlesex, England.

RECORDS

To save the spellbinding material in the rest of the book from being broken up by a lot of other records, some of which may no longer exist, and to avoid dating the book (we want your grandchildren to read it, too), we have put this bundle of present records in a separate section. Thus, if you abhor records and things, as some of us do, you may ignore this section. Or if the records become out-dated, you can simply tear out this section before passing the book on in a few years time to the grandkids. There are some characters around who love and live with the game and know vital facts like how often Jim Pike sharpened his points (you did hear that his stance was side-on to the hockey, didn't you?), and to these types, records are like atoms to a reactor.

The following are other feats of dartability: You can practice by having a few trial shots at them, but as we say, not all are world records but all are impressive accomplishments.

* Two lads from Yorkshire, England, claim a new world record for scoring 1,410,642 in 48 hours of throwing, with a total of 2 hours rest.

* Martin Adams in a solo marathon set two records at the Suffolk Punch, Milton Keynes. After 10 hours of continuous throwing, Martin set a ten hour solo record of 193,149 (an average of 25.63 per dart). Tired Martin went on to finish a 24 hour marathon with a score of 402,173 (an average of 23.34 per dart). In total, he threw 17,229 darts. 34 of these throws were 180's.

* A two man 24 hour record was recently established by Kevin Cross and Richard Heathcote when they recorded a total score of 618,762.

* In the Mixed Pairs category, Malcolm Winters and Sandra Pellow (at the Cutty Sark, Marazion Corn-well) set an eight hour record score of 229,171. 21 180's were registered.

* For the Ladies, a 12 hour marathon record score of 282,471 was recently recorded by eight attractive, but tired sweethearts at the George, Swindon.

* A solo performance was set by Steve Foster of Keighley, West Yorkshire, when he scored 132,841 in six hours.

* Not to be outdone, Mrs. Sue Arnett of Macclesfield, Chesire, set a new high for the women's six hour marathon with a score of 85,845.

* An eight man team from the Royal Berkshire Hospital Social Club of Reading gathered 368,708 points during a 12 hour marathon — beating the old standing record by almost 26,000.

* The golden 1,000,001 is the big challenge. Present target is claimed at 9 hours 27 minutes and 35 seconds by a 16 member team from the Skinner's Arms pub in Surrey, England. Tension, tension, tension . . . it took 49 darts to get the last double.

* Another claim for a world record is by Denny Gower of England who scored 200 doubles in 49 minutes and 6.9 seconds.

* The marathon darts record, as in the *Guiness Book of Records* set in 1973 by a four man team from Kent, England, took almost fifteen days and nights. They threw 314,530 darts.

* The 2,000,001 record stands at 71 hours 24 minutes for a four man team from Birmingham, England. They scored a ton or over 5,002 times.

* 180, the darts players Nirvana, was scored 62 times in a 1,000,001 darts marathon by six players from Staffordshire, England, during an attempt at the record.

* Dennis Bernhard, playing out of the Crest in Torrance, California, has never won a game in five years of dart play. When asked how he was able to establish this record, his only comment was, "I don't know, I just can't put my finger on it."

The End

About the Authors:

WILLIAM FITZGERALD

Popularly known as "Big Bird" or "The Machine" among his friends and enemies. This good looking genius has travelled the world over during the past twelve years seeking out darts challenges. For the past five years Big Bird has been a resident of Japan having decided by experience that the world's magnetic pull five feet eight inches from sea level is strongest in Tokyo. His rare losses in games are usually attributed to someone cheating. In twelve years of darts play "The Machine" has racked up four perfect games of 301, three times has scored three in the double Bull and has three in the treble 20 bed down to a bad habit. Big Bird is married and between games has managed to have three children.

IVAN BRACKIN

Started playing darts as a Boy Scout almost twenty years ago and despite many attempts to quit has still not managed to chuck the habit.

Of his many famous feats on the dartboard the most memorable was when he whitewashed a fellow at a game of 301 throwing only a sharpened electrician's screwdriver.

The arrows of outrageous fortune have stuck him with a brood of three daughters (none of who play darts) and a double jointed darts thumb that bends backwards at 90°.

Since leaving England in 1963 he has wandered through some twenty-six countries in search of the perfect darts partner. He met Big Bird three years ago and they have thrown happily together ever since.

INDEX

INDEX